AFTERM

BUSINESS AFTER THE GREAT PAUSE

by LINKED IN AND TOWN HALL ACHIEVER OF THE YEAR

EY NOMINEE ENTREPRENEUR OF THE YEAR

GRAND HOMAGE LYS DIVERSITY

Dr. BAK NGUYEN, DMD

&

by TWO TIMES LAUREATE DUNAMIS

HOMAGE QUEBEC DENTISTS ORDER

TELUS SOCIAL IMPLICATION AWARD

Dr. ERIC LACOSTE,
BSc, DMD, MSc, F.R.C.D(C), MBA

TO ALL THOSE WHO RUN AND MANAGE
CORPORATIONS, BIG ORGANIZATIONS
THINKERS AND PHILANTHROPISTS .

by Dr. BAK NGUYEN
& Dr. ERIC LACOSTE

ISBN: 978-1-989536-38-4

AFTERMATH

BUSINESS AFTER THE GREAT PAUSE

by Dr. BAK NGUYEN
& Dr. ERIC LACOSTE

INTRODUCTION
BY Dr. BAK NGUYEN

INTRODUCTION
BY Dr. ERIC LACOSTE

THE TSUNAMI
CHAPTER 1 - Dr. BAK NGUYEN

EMOTIONS: THE POWERFUL DRIVER INSIDE
CHAPTER 2 - Dr. ERIC LACOSTE

THE SHIELD
CHAPTER 3 - Dr. BAK NGUYEN

WE ALL SMILE IN THE SAME LANGUAGE
CHAPTER 4 - Dr. ERIC LACOSTE

TOO BIG TO FAIL?
CHAPTER 5 - Dr. BAK NGUYEN

YOU CAN'T GO TO WAR IF YOU CAN'T FINANCE IT
CHAPTER 6 - Dr. ERIC LACOSTE

GOOD BUSINESS SENSE
CHAPTER 7 - Dr. BAK NGUYEN

CONCLUSION

MY PLEA
BY Dr. BAK NGUYEN

INTRODUCTION

by Dr. BAK NGUYEN

As I write these words, I am confined within my soul… and my home. It's been a few weeks that I have to live with social distancing and a quarantine life pace. Not that I've committed any crime, but a virus is eating up the world and its economy.

I am a dentist and I have been ordered to cease all not urgent care. Well, I am a cosmetic dentist and take pretty good care of our patients, 99% of my treatments are under control and do not qualify as medical emergencies. Even the skyscraper in which my clinic is located is in lockdown. I had no other choice than to be home, waiting for this crisis to pass.

This comes at an odd time as Tranie, my wife and business partner was scheduled for an operation for her back. She was amongst the last people in surgery before the new guideline of the health minister to postpone all none life treating surgeries. Her operation still required 3 months of convalescence. We had plans and hired the help. But within this crisis, the task falls to me.

I did my best, but I am a doctor, not a nurse. It is now that I appreciate every person for their role in the system. No one is above nor below anybody else, I now understand the weight of those words. That took much of my attention for the last 2 weeks.

As I was about to resume my clinical duties, the news came like crashing thunder, we will remain close for another 5 weeks! The first 2 were rough, but another 5?! That will put most of the dental clinics and me out of business! And what about my staff? Those people I work with on a daily basis?

They all call me in panic, not knowing what will happen. The governments are doing a tremendous effort fighting an invisible enemy hidden within any of us. I could ignore the truth anymore, the virus was only the first wave. After it, the recession is following and will hit all of us hard, dentists, patients, businesses and employees.

The forecast was pointing out that the virus could conservatively kill about 1% of the population. On the other hand, the first estimates were saying that about 25% of the small businesses might not survive the second wave, the recession. The stock market already crashed a few times at the time of this writing.

All around the world, the governments put everything on pause mode, to keep people home to contain the virus from spreading. Well, most of the population obey the directives. All the war efforts were at the enemy, **THE VIRUS**.

I couldn't stay put. My staff was still waiting for confirmation of some sort of financial support. The government announced many measures, but nothing was clear yet. Before shutting down Mdex, I did promise my staff that I would be there for them.

On this **dark Monday**, I didn't know what else to do, but to go on camera and to reaffirm that I will stand by their side in this time of crisis. In the effort to help them and all the others in their situation, I took my phone and started dialling the ministers and influential people I knew.

To my surprise, all of them took the call or returned my call. I offered my help to assist in this crisis and to help my industry (which has been shot down 2 weeks earlier than the rest of the population) through these troubled times.

Be careful at what you wish for! Within hours, I had two initiatives up, one to help save our economy and the other to save the dental industry.

Yes, I know too clearly what is coming: with a recession post-virus, dentists are not losing a month or two in production, but half, if not the entire year, since everyone will have to catch up and make up for their loss in this crisis; if they still have a job to go back to. Dental cares, just like the governments decreed, will be at the bottom of their priorities.

I am not crying nor complaining, I am forecasting the future of my industry. I got my point across as I was the intermediary in the backchannels of communication between governments and officials. (Sorry, I cannot be any more precise due to confidences agreement).

So as 25% of small businesses might not survive this crisis, my industry is made of 70 to 85% of small businesses! That means that most of my industry is in peril! That's why I stood up and raised my voice.

My goal was to connect the industry and to reach different leaders all across the world to mobilize a common front.

"For the first time of our lifetime,
all the interests of the world are aligned."
Dr. Bak Nguyen

There is no more competition anymore, we are all in this together! During this unique times, I was close to the president of the dentists association of Quebec, Dr. Carl Tremblay. Despite his best efforts to address the issues of the dental industry and having the support of a favorable press, it backfired.

On social media, people were criticizing the article and even went as far as to insult his views. I was speechless. While I was receiving encouragement and support from my own patients, both verbally and in writing, my profession did not have good press.

What I saw, the governments and the population did too. We have no voice, within a few comments on social media after a favorable press article, we were left voiceless to raise our concerns and needs. This is an entire industry we are talking about, many families, jobs and all the patients needing our cares: the nation.

Maybe, but later. This was the main message. I was sad, but this was not the time to cry over the scars. If anything, it flamed the passion in me. I went online and start writing to my connections, to leader across the world to join me for interviews, via teleconference.

I also called some of my influential friends and *"forced"* their hands to have their participation. All responded, some with an interview and some from proposing their help behind the scene. I am grateful and respect that not everyone likes to be in the eye of the public.

If there is one thing they learned about me, is that as crazy as I may sound, I will do it and do it in a big way! So yes, I understood those who preferred to help behind, far from the the lighting and the cameras.

I interviewed formers head of banks, celebrities, high ranking loans officers, entrepreneurs and leaders in the dental field. Amongst them, Dr. Eric Lacoste stood out for a second interview.

While everybody was talking about the economy, about saving jobs, about finding ways to resume dentistry and save the industry, Dr. Lacoste was talking about those philanthropic initiatives he was supporting. He is a community leader helping kids.

From his own words, he will find a way through this crisis, but he is worried about those he was helping and what to come with them, now that most people will be looking at their own survival. I must admit, even if I was working for a better future for all, my aim and intelligence were on the economy and the jobs, not philanthropy.

But Dr. Lacoste is right, in this time of crisis, the most vulnerable are also the first casualties. I kept it for myself, but listening to the man speaking with genuine passion, I felt shame. I proposed a way to incorporate his thinking into the plan to relaunch our industry. I made a plan covering from the resuming of all dental practice via **TELE-DENTISTRY**, the welcoming back of all our staff members to making the most out of this crisis, banking on our continuous education credits, I even included the help to our universities to avoid the postponing of the graduates in the dental field.

On the last point, an interview with Professor Thomas Nguyen from Harvard pointed out that all last year dental candidates might not graduate with the suspension of their clinical duties. Because I was profoundly moved by Dr. Lacoste, I included a component of treating those left most vulnerable in this crisis and those who have given much within this crisis.

Well, the video and the plan spread throughout on the web as wildfire. Those leaders I interviewed all wrote back to know how we could make this work. It might not be the best plan, but we had no alternatives.

Within all the return, guess who wanted a phone conversation? Dr. Eric Lacoste. He loved the passion and the social impact, but moreover, he felt something familiar, the genuine wish to make the world a better place.

Within minutes, he convinced me to interview someone else, Mylène Du Bois, CEO of a child preventive care unit. Together, they made their case in an interview and convinced me of the urge to act.

I am momentum and leverage, my mind is working to find and to apply leverage. I lent them my brain for the rest of the afternoon. Usually, I operate at a whole other level, even in philanthropy, but their genuine passion got the best of me.

I know that through this crisis, the world will never be the same again. Years ago, as I was coached to run in politic, my coach and mentor taught me the orientation of the United Nations and the importance of corporate citizenship, socially involved.

It was a great speech and great ideas, but a corporation could do well even without embracing those noble values. Well, not anymore, in this time of age, all industries have been rebooted. By the time that we unpause the economy, everybody will be in critical condition and looking for customers, governments grants and help.

Just like what happened with the backfire of the article about the dental industry, those organizations without social support might not get the needed help or will have to stand in line, hoping that there is still money left.

No, all dentists will not disappear. But it was the example I needed to understand the challenge we face, not only as an industry but as a society. As I said, before, many structures and organizations are inherited from the industrialization age. Even if they have updated with the years, with this reboot, a firmware upgrade is needed in the best case. In the other cases, we might need a change in operating system, to use an imagery easy to understand.

I will lead the way for my industry, but it became clearer that I might need to do more, to help all industries to embrace the passion of Dr. Lacoste, to put at their core, a social component. Not solely from the goodness of their heart, that's Dr. Lacoste charisma speaking. I know leverage, because if they do not, they will be replaced, and sooner than they might think!

I am not judging anyone. If anything, it took me years to understand my coaching and teaching to become a leader. Now, I am doing this because I can, because I know and because I care.

The United Nations talked about this for years now. With **THE REBOOT**, now is the time to upgrade our economy to match the information era, the millennials and the advent of socio media. Yes, today, a teenager with a smartphone and a connection can beat a multi-million dollar public relation campaign! What do you do with that?

This book is merely the beginning and the planning of the new world economy, one that will impose itself by itself at the **AFTERMATH** of **THE VIRUS**.

Within the following pages, I will join forces with Dr. Lacoste to help you ease your transition, and, yes, to make the world a better place!

"In time of crisis, it is the perfect opportunity to reinvent who we are. "

Dr. Bak Nguyen

This is **AFTERMATH - BUSINESS AFTER THE GREAT PAUSE.**

In time of crisis,
It is the perfect opportunity
To reinvent who we are.
Dr. BAK NGUYEN

INTRODUCTION

by Dr. ERIC LACOSTE

Though this only would become clear to me at a much later age, I was, since a very young always, driven by two things:

- The desire to excel
- The genuine sense to care for others

Little did I know, these two characteristics would define most of who I am today. Though I will expose who I am in this book, I will say that who I am, brings me to fundamentally believe that true entrepreneurial success should never be dissociated from **empathy** and from corporate social responsibility.

During my school years, I lived a few years at the house of my aunt, Marie Josée and uncle Emile Ollivier. My uncle was a successful writer who won several prestigious awards for his work. He passed away a few years back. My aunt significantly contributed to my uncle's work before writing a book herself.

Imagine the pressure on me to step into this arena. I do not have the audacity to call myself a writer but I believe that my message is important. If I do not write, I will leave things unchanged, unchallenged.

This is not about style, it's about speaking from the heart. This is about experiences and more importantly, it is a perspective on what our future could be in light of unprecedented events.

My uncle had a home office. It was a sizable room that had shelves full of books from floor to ceiling. There was no way you could not feel intellectually motivated when you sat in that room. This is where I took the love for reading, and now, writing a book about the initiative that we have implemented for the children.

In these troubled times, where **THE VIRUS** threatens to change humanity as we know, I say that the timing could not be better to consider new and better ways, not only to do business, but also to take care of each other, especially the most vulnerable of our society.

Reaching out to friends, business relations, and connecting with whoever would be willing to hear me out. I started to post more on LinkedIn. I strongly believe that there is a lot of power in understanding other's journey to help creating a journey of your own.

My first post said " **THE VIRUS** day one: Waking up this morning we must remember that planet earth is the only residence for the human race. In light of this pandemic, we realize that the planet is much smaller than we could have ever imagined and that our common destiny is far more interdependent that we wanted to believe. Let's stand united and not be selfish. Let's us show what humanity can accomplish. It is our future in the making.

I sent this post like a message in a bottle. It collected a respectable 6000 views and was well-liked. To me, this was a sign that many others felt the need to connect. People came from all horizons, business owners, journalists, lawyers, dentists, directors, teachers, city workers, and many others.

Within that group, maybe some would be willing to join a movement where we would work together to generate new ideas and new ways of doing thing across industries and around the planet.

Call me irrational, but I think that between meteorological disasters, devastating earthquakes, wildfires in Australia not to mention all the other problems we are so familiar with like hunger, war and now another super virus, mother earth is talking to us, and she is not happy.

My idea of creating a new way of doing things and especially of doing business is not new to me. A few years ago, I made a few futile attempts to write to world-renowned personalities such as former president Barak Obama or formula one's world champion, Lewis Hamilton, with the hope that my letter (in a bottle) would reach them, and that maybe, they would help me carry out the ideas with their unique power of influence. To no surprise of mine, it did not work.

At the end of the day, I am just a periodontist. In other words, a very small fish in the sea. Connecting with whoever would be willing to hear me out. It is then that I meet a unique individual, Dr. Bak Nguyen, a visionary man who shared my point of view on the dental industry and how we, as an industry, could adapt in the **aftermath** of **THE VIRUS**. I was humbled by his request, and three conversations later, we started a friendship and this book happened.

"In rare moments opportunity presents itself unannounced, grab it when it is there!"
Dr. Eric Lacoste

So I did, I grabbed the opportunity. The vision I will describe is, in essence, quite simple and maybe even sounds too simplistic for some, but remain too often underused, considering the amount of concrete and positive results it generates.

In this chapter, I will share with you what I do and why I do it. This with the modest hope, that others will replicate and improve my model. If so, maybe we could create sustainable changes and an innovative business model so that the world could become a better place!

THE WHY

As I reached professional success with my private practice and as a real estate investor, I was still left with an inexplicable void inside. Was I sick? After all, I was comfortable, and I was building my own version of the so-called **AMERICAN DREAM**, on my way to accumulate appreciable financial wealth.

Don't get me wrong, I love fancy cars and trips to the world's most beautiful destinations, but my genuine care for others was there inside of me, growing and pushing me to take on a different path.

At the time, I had the urge to participate in humanitarian missions in Haiti, amongst initiatives. In the grand scheme of things, those were very punctual interventions with very little impact on the long term. Nonetheless, that chapter of my journey enlightened me on the fact that is helping those in need.

Then one day, during the course of my MBA studies, I read a book titled **BUSINESS AND SOCIETY ETHICS AND STAKEHOLDER MANAGEMENT**, by Len Karakowsky, Archie

Carrol and Ann Buchholtz. The second chapter was named Corporate Citizenship. It enlightened me and helped me to identify that void I felt inside.

I sat down and start thinking. Within a few nights, I clarified my vision, what I needed to achieve, the people I wanted to help and the actions I needed to take from that point on. Mainly, I end up with a hope and the draft of a plan.

Keeping my track record and adding the philanthropy now as a key component of my vision, I knew that I was going to be successful, but I was hoping to gain influence along the way. I would use it for the benefit of my community, most specifically its most vulnerable members.

I am not a fan of half measures, my initiative required structures and would need to generate measurable and sustainable results. This is how I started building, on the field.

THE HOW: FIND A WAY

In its most simple expression, I needed to do two things. First to lead by example and two, to spread the message to create awareness. That's exactly what I did.

"To always find a way..."
Dr. Eric Lacoste

That simple sentence resonates in my mind. I started to look at my company with new questions in mind:

(Phase 1)

Could I allocate some financial resources differently so that I could accomplish more while maintaining the same profitability?

(Phase 2)

How could I maximize the allocated resources to maximize dollar value?

(Phase 3)

How could I mobilize stakeholders to join the movement without alienating them? This needed to be sustainable in the long term.

Simple answers came to all these questions, and with this I was able to set up and execute my plan. Then, **THE VIRUS** happened.

"The strongest individuals find ways to help others, even when they are struggling themselves."
Dr. Eric Lacoste

On March 15th 2020, the Quebec Health Minister and the different boards in the dental field requested the closure of all dental offices except for medical emergencies. With this, my revenues went flat to absolute zero and most of my financial means to help my community were gone with it.

Call me lunatic, but I am honestly not so worried about the financial impact of this crisis on my practice. Yes, it will be a very difficult year, and the worst-case scenario includes bankruptcy. But for as long as I am healthy, my kids Olivier, Matis and Nathan will inspire me to be the best version of myself, each and every day. I will be fine. I will find a way, I always do!

I am more concerned about the most vulnerable ones. In time of abundance, I support them and encourage those I know to join my efforts. But now, in the midst of a global crisis, the needs of those children (that's my cause), is not reduced. If anything, they need more help now than ever! That last thought kept haunting me every time I close my eyes. I need to find a way!

How can I keep the public attention and the awareness so we will keep our support to those in need, those members living in my community, miles away from my own home?

Then, talking with Dr. Bak, the opportunity to write this book came as a mean to humbly sharing my vision and approach on why corporate social responsibility should be a core component of any long term successful business model.

I have great hope that the world will contribute to help one another and contribute to design a new and better business model, a new business class, in the light of the lessons learned during these challenging times.

Did I ever matter? At the end of my journey, my hope is that I mattered to someone, that I've changed his/her destiny for the better. If so, I will have truly made a difference to improve someone else's life, and that will be my legacy and accomplishment.

I hope to accomplish enough as to leave absolutely no doubt to the question: did I ever matter?

"Simple ideas can lead to great results"
Dr. Eric Lacoste

In time of crisis,
It is the perfect opportunity
To reinvent who we are.
Dr. BAK NGUYEN

CHAPTER 1
"THE TSUNAMI"
by Dr. BAK NGUYEN

THE VIRUS hit us hard, very hard, way deeper than we know. What started as flash news on TV and posts on social media, resonated as a foreign infection in a country far far away.

The media were all over it, but just like anything else, we were immune to the media storm; they are looking to regain their lost popularity and attention. That's what so many of us thought.

Should it be a ban on traveling, on cruise ships? Should we ban importation from the infected countries? The sound of the ideas in themselves was apocalyptic, alarmist and simply too far stretched to even make it into a Hollywood script, not the infection, but our possible reaction to it. And we all went our ways and our lives as usual.

As a society, we've grown into tolerating many changes and dangers before changing our ways.

"Changing is never something
we welcome easily."
Dr. Bak Nguyen

Have we lost our sensitivity, our ability to adapt? This is an answer that we will soon find out, now that we are backed against the wall of confinement from an invisible enemy. The virus is just the first wave.

A dark flu that is taking away our wisdom. It is jumping from individual to individual without much warming. It is ironic how we have grown to be individuals walking side by side in a collective and yet, are that affected by a virus transmitting through contact. From a society standpoint, we built bridges and hubs to act, move and live as one, not together, but as one.

"The paradox of our evolution is to have grown into a collective of individuals."
Dr. Bak Nguyen

That's how the virus sneaked in, while we are sitting next to one another, focused on our little LCD pocket screen, connected to the virtual world. We were side by side, and still, we never saw or simply ignore.

On the other hand, the planet has never been that small, all those flagged collectives networking with one another. We built and built, spread out and reached further and further, one following another, one racing the other to know who is going to dominate the markets and the world.

That's on one hand. On the other hand, for as long as the distribution process was efficient and stable, many of our institutions never had to evolve. Sure, they adapted their distribution and production mechanisms to match the global competition, and then, let the numbers drive their evolution and growth.

Recessions and economic contractions? Well, those are now like the storms and hurricanes hitting the Caribbean sea and Florida; they are to be expected. Has some people might lose their lives, we will prevail, as a country, a species, and we will rebuild and heal.

Well, we will, even after **THE VIRUS Tsunami**. But this virus will have changed our lives and, our prosperity; our complacency and our views of the world forever.

As the dolphins are coming back in Venice, while the tourists have banned the airports and the Venetians are confined home, is it the purge of the modern age, how God is destroying Babylon, once again?

We stood tall, we build high, and we grew confident, arrogant. Now, we are way passed the arrogance, we grew complacent, thinking that we are forever. This is a **REBOOT** of all the systems, of the whole system, and it happens all at once. We were never prepared for such a reboot.

Since the last great war, we built a new global economy, one without borders. We built bridges instead of walls. Even those built, lasted for a few decades and crumbled down. Those bridges we built expanded our horizons and economy. They allowed many our us to open our mind. Diversity became a trend and a new reality.

"To grow, one must open their mind.
That the start. To not stay stuck, one also
has to open their heart too."
Dr. Bak Nguyen & William Bak

This is where we are coming from, where we stood a few weeks earlier. Now the virus has spread in the center of our human hub. Within weeks, it has traveled the world from our complacency and connectivity, safe thanks to our individualism and immunity to alarmists.

It has reached our core. As we are confined home, we are forced to face the creation that we've built through our choices, greed, fear and complacency. Now that everything is on pause, that nature is taking back over, that time is suddenly universal, we have a choice to made: to adapt or to disappear. Can we still do that?

That the real Tsunami, the virus was only the catalyst starting a chained reaction. The recession coming is of **biblical proportions** if we do not act fast. Make no mistake, if we do not take drastic means, the world will not recuperate from this crisis for a long time.

Why? Simply because this crisis put all economies on the same foot. If everyone is underwater, no one will be left to pull the other one out. If we can react quickly, can we rebuild and upgrade while in pause, so we will limit the casualties and damages?

Am I an apocalyptic prophet looking for fame, feeding our the growing collective fear? Absolutely not, if anything, I was a none believer of **THE VIRUS** and the apocalyptic scenarios until lately. Now, backed against my wall in confinement, I am forced to reacted drastically and to adapt quickly. So no, I am not judging nor blaming anyone. I am trying to make up for all our complacency.

"Big deal, the economy will take over as soon as we have the upper hand on the virus, and better times are coming. All that we have to do will be to make up for the lost time." This is what our complacency is telling us. Not this time. Never in the History of the modern world, all the economies stopped and stood still all at once.

Even in times of war, as one country is ravaged, the other ones had their factories running day and night to keep up the war effort. Then, it was the rebuilding. Again, full employment! In this **COVID war**, there is no war economy, just the fear and the siege.

At war, there are spoils of war for the victorious. In a siege, the victory is survival with an aftertaste of fear and scars. It has been only a few weeks, most of the planet is still in shock, in denial or in stupefaction. But, mark my words, the awakening won't be a smooth one.

As all the eyeballs are focused the body count and the infected, **FEAR** will soon take over all of us while we are idle. This is the real treat, **FEAR**.

What brought down the walls, one after the next, was **GREED**, our envy for more and more, good greed, bad greed, but still, greed. Now that **FEAR** has a chance to govern the world once again, **HATE** and **PROTECTIONIST** will be the next trends, in the name of our survival!

We must not enter such a path. This is a **REBOOT**, a forced and unplanned reboot of all of our systems. Sure, we will have to see what's left after the reboot and what will need to be replaced, but as Sir Winston Churchill said standing under the raining of bombs:

"If you think that you are going through hell, keep going!"
Sir Winston Churchill

That our only way to keep our way of life and our hardly gain freedom. To avoid a global tsunamic recession, we must stay away from **FEAR**. To resist closing, even more, our hearts and minds as we will be slowly clamming back the surface of our old realms and kingdoms.

Stay away from **FEAR** and panic, just like you've resisted eating the toilet's paper from the shelves! Our forefathers and foremothers have sacrificed too much for us to behave as such.

"The only way to avoid a global recession is to expand our openness and connectivity, not retracting them!"
Dr. Bak Nguyen

Think with me, if all the jobs are maintained, after this forced confinement, most people will resume their complacency and **FEAR** will have lost root and the war! To do so, our decision-makers will have to produce even if the immediate logic of numbers and profits will say otherwise.

To keep all the jobs and the full employment is not a cure, but a mean to defeat a second infection, the reign of **FEAR**. On that, our officials are leading the way, to save our economy. Well, we do not want to save our economy because it won't be enough.

We need to expand our economy, not from **GREED**, but to win the race against the **AFTERMATH of THE VIRUS**. As I said in the beginning of this book: for the first time of our lifetime, all interest aligned!

We all know that the world has changed forever and that our complacency is over. At least, we can all agree on something.

PHASE ONE: take away the power from **FEAR** and avoid panic. People got the message, and they will be responding. For this to work, we must keep all the jobs in place, so people can have the hope to resume their lives. This will avoid the panic and the amplification of the viral damages.

PHASE TWO: we need to expand our economy as quickly as possible. Just like the aftermath of a war, we need to rebuild, but only this time, nothing has been demolished by bombs. Well, the alternative is to play catch up and to understand later on that we had no chance of marching uphill, against the wind of **FEAR** with the usual means. Our response will have to be a muscular one, maybe even one without precedent.

"Make leverage out of each of your liability to thrive. Survival isn't the only option."
Dr. Bak Nguyen

Since this is artificial and that we are building with the horizon to fight **FEAR**, we will also need to build differently. No enterprise or organization will be able to do so without the help of the central powers.

Nowadays, the central powers are closer and closer to the people. How can you keep all the jobs when you are losing money? But if all of the business class is joining, with the help of governments, we have a shot! On that, the courage of our leaders is to not rewrite the rules but to write History itself.

Even if we win that siege against **THE VIRUS** and the war against **FEAR**, we cannot simply let **GREED** solely in control. **GREED** can be a great motivator, but if our governments are investing and mortgaging the collective future in the hope of an even better one, we will need to outdo ourself.

20 years ago, an initiative from the **United Nations** called the **UN Global Compact** was formed with the goal to level the field between the richest and those in need. Well, this is our chance, maybe our only hope to gain something out of this war. To leave no child, woman or man behind. Yes, it is a dream, but it is a noble one.

If you want a chance to have the ear of our central powers, to have the favor of the crowd to expand from this unprecedented economic pause, you need to expand not only your scope and your ambition, but you also need to open your heart as never before.

In simple words, try to resume business as usual, and you will fail. Try to ask for government financial help, since all will be doing the same, you might wait in line for little or nothing, and maybe it will come too late.

This is the situation of an industry I know all too well, a maybe small industry, but none the less, an essential one: the dental industry. I am not basing my reflections on how we look at teeth, but this industry is an example of what to come if we chose to close our eyes and heart and to try to resume business as usual.

As you know, everyone is suffering from financial losses as the virus is prospering. Well, the dental industry was the first one to react, closing their activity 2 weeks prior to the rest of the world. As they did so to protect the public, they did not have the general favor of the crowd.

The governments saw that too. As a result, the whole industry was left without much attention nor financial help. I know, I am leading the charge to save my industry, and I am texting with minister and officials… I arrived at such conclusions while they are taking the time in the midst of this crisis to return my texts and calls. Even with such influence, I can barely see the light.

We arrived at this point even if we take care of people on a daily basis. We are doctors, and we are taking care of people, doing good and no harm. Many of my colleagues and myself have emails and phone calls of support from our patients, but that's only on a personal level. As an industry, we do not have the favor of the crowd, and will we suffer for it.

As I met with Dr. Lacoste, we both reached at the conclusion that the only way to rewrite the public perception was from within: we have to be more listening to the pains and desires of the public. I promise you, I am addressing those issues as I am writing these lines.

If dentists can't stand in the public imagination to contribute somehow to the good of the community, even if they are servicing it with all their skills, they will be left behind. And so will you!

Learn from the misfire, the lack of leadership and vision of this industry to save yours! It is not too late, while we are in pause and that our governments are listening, you have the chance to rebuild the core of your business with the genuine idea of caring for others, of being a good corporate citizen.

How can you do that? Well, I can tell you what I am doing with **Mdex & Co**, leading the charge to change the world from a dental chair. As I am providing a way out of this crisis to dentists, a way that will lead to their freedom, wealth and happiness, I will also ask of each and every one of them, 5% of their time and 2% of their profit reinvested in society, philanthropy. Not only in respond of this crisis, but as a core DNA of our partnership, the new economic model proposed to reform my industry into a community of responsible and proper individuals.

This is also printed in our proposal to the investors, banks and governments as we are closing down on our financing. This is a huge risk to take for a company like mine, but I asked myself, am I a leader or not?

"Leading is not about power, it s about courage."
Dr. Bak Nguyen

This is the right thing to do, but before, I wasn't sensitive enough to it. I wasn't courageous enough. I built and reinvested all of myself, all my life. This crisis can wipe me out in an instant. Just like Dr. Lacoste, I'll be fine, I'll find a way, I always do. But will my team, my staff, will all of you?

I am asking you to look beyond your immediate needs for a moment to grasp the seriousness of the situation. We all have the chance to make a stand and to refuse to bow down to this virus and to fear. Will you open your heart to expand your impact, your company, your organization?

The alternative is simply to resume our **GREED** and **AMBITION** and to hope that this is just a bad dream. It is not, and the bad dream can still turn into a nightmare.

The Tsunami has yet to reach our shore. But for the first time in History, we know what's coming, when it is coming and how to face it. Usually, like princess Cassandra, the voice of the prophet is not heard, even if it was nothing but true.

Well, the prophet, this time, came in the shape of a virus, **THE VIRUS**. This time, everyone listened. And the prophet is not the cataclysm itself, but only the precursor and the messenger.

But think of it, for a minute, how does a virus work? It is a partial DNA code that infiltrates a host and use its structure to reproduce and to rewrite the future. Well, the virus has infected our society, body and economy.

Will we let it rewrite our minds and hearts too? Actually, the answer to that question is futile since it has already reached our minds, and the rewriting process has already begun.

The only question left is will we let the virus do as it sees fit, or will we rewrite our code and core ourselves?

"Choose complacency and fear, and you will have forfeit your voice and freedom!"
Dr. Bak Nguyen

Will you forfeit your great city of TROY or will you build a greater one? So many heroes haven't fallen for us to stand where we are. We can rise as heroes and victors out of this one? Only if we expand our heart and stand together, as one.

Oh, and just before I finish this chapter, ignore this and you will soon be living in regrets, holding on to a past that no longer exists. You can blame the virus and fate, but you were given the choice and the chance. Remember that.

"Adapt or disappear, this is your choice."
Dr. Bak Nguyen

This is the information age, the rise of the millennials and the reign of social media.

This is **AFTERMATH - BUSINESS AFTER THE GREAT PAUSE.**

In time of crisis,
It is the perfect opportunity
To reinvent who we are.
Dr. BAK NGUYEN

CHAPTER 2

"EMOTIONS: THE POWERFUL DRIVE INSIDE"

by Dr. ERIC LACOSTE

At first glance, anyone close to me would describe me as being very calm, composed and in control by nature. They will also tell you that my brain and my heart are strongly connected. I am a very emotional person, and with time, I learned to channel these emotions to use them as a powerful source of energy.

The will to do certain things is often not enough. Intervening in the life of an underprivileged individual requires knowledge, experience and expertise. The wrong intervention, even with the best intentions, can lead to catastrophic results.

Les Cayes, Haiti summer 2000, lessons learned

This was my first real humanitarian mission. Fresh out of my general practice residency completed at the Albany Medical Center New York. I was ready to tackle any challenges!

I joined a medical/dental mission supported by the Gaskov Clergé Foundation. According to various sources, Haiti ranks 18 out of 25 among the poorest countries in the world and the number 1 in the

Americas. Statistically, approximately 46% of the population suffers from malnutrition.

The need for help and the lack of resources appear infinite. The city of Les Cayes is no exception. It is where my mother was born before she immigrated to Canada.

We set up and operated a mobile clinic under conditions that were beyond imagination. So we went on to help patient number 1, number 10, number 100… I simply lost count. I also lost a part of myself there. The needs were overwhelming.

With the best intentions, we provided toothbrushes, toothpastes, dental floss and oral hygiene instructions. Most of the items we gave were on sale the very next day at the local street market. I guess it made sense when you can make a profit and have something to eat! Eat first, then, brush your teeth!

After two full days of treating patients from sunrise to sunset, I started thinking that we were too slow and that we needed to move up the pace. So I pushed my team, hard.

We did more screening which led to more demand for treatments putting more stress on the staff and our limited resources. I skipped breaks and even lunches to see more people. That seemed to be the only thing that I can do, more!

Actually, I was giving my share of the provided lunch for the kids who were clearly hungrier than I was. Me, I was hungry to help, more! The problem is that after a few lunches, 2 kids became 5 and then 10 and then I could get no more additional food.

It started to happen: sterilization could not keep up with our needs. There were far more patients waiting in line than we were ever going to be able to see and care for. Even the most resilient ones were growing impatient. You can picture the chaotic situation that I pushed for, with the best of intentions.

We did our best, and we helped as many as we could. I was not alone, but I felt responsible because I was the one pushing. I followed my heart and passion, but along the way, I deviated from the plan because the plan could not meet the demand.

"I don't like the word compassion,
as it resembles to a label."
Dr. Eric Lacoste

To be truly effective in delivering help, you must respect the limits of your means, and you must have a team of experts. If you don't, the likelihood of failure is very high, too high.

Partnering with the right experts and developing the right partnership became of utmost importance. With this combination, I could drive my passion while gaining in efficiency within the safeguards.

That's how a new business deal was created. One where I promised to find a way, to share my financial resources and my business relations in counterpart of a deal that would hold them accountable for the diligent management of my contribution.

With this, it became possible for us to control allocated resources with the same diligence that we are managing our own inventory.

"Trust does not exclude supervision."
Dr. Eric Lacoste

The system has its limits.

If you wait for the system to fix a problem that does not affect the majority, there is a significant probability that the problem will become irretrievable! So if you truly want to implement change, you must take matters in your own hands and made that change yourself, not hope and wait for them.

At this point of my life, I knew I was going to support the cause of underprivileged children. I also knew what I would demand from the experts receiving my support, means and ideas. It was time for action.

After a few trials and errors with organizations that simply did not have the seriousness to commit to us the same way we committed to them, we established a partnership with the Social Paediatric Center of Laval who provides consistent cares for approximately 300 children.

All of this, at this point, may sound trivial. After all, so many other people have so many good ideas to contribute locally. Yet as the story unfolds, you will see the emergence a new way of thinking, a new dream and vision lining up with the world's largest corporate sustainability, initiative presented by the United Nations.

Caught up in my own reality, I had no idea that the UN created such initiative. Our paths simply did not cross. We have much work to do if we hope that this message to be universal.

An ocean starts with a single water drop. Maybe today this realization is the one of a simple periodontist with a big conscience, but if we walk together, we could change the world.

The first step, a simple Band-aid !

Christmas should be time of the year for every child. What else is there to add? While the very meaning of Christmas is probably drowned by industrialization and consumption by our modern societies, the meaning of a Christmas gift is a part of our culture. Every child should get one.

At its simplest expression, it allows them not to feel excluded and more importantly, it shows that someone thought of you whoever that maybe! This is how and why I promised that I would fight for this and that all children part of my engagement would get a personalized gift.

Whether it came for Santa Claus or anybody else does not matter. The magical feeling you get when you receive a box wrapped and the excitement to open a surprise creates unique moments in the youth of a child. Soon enough, these children will grow into adults and join our collective stress. My hopes is that they got something to build from, that innocence of a happy child!

Back in 2008, I wrote a letter to all of the professionals and colleagues I usually thanked at Christmas with a bottle of wine, chocolate etc, telling them that I would use this money to buy Christmas gifts for children who otherwise would get none.

The idea was generally very well received. With my team and with my children, we went to work buying and rapping countless Christmas gifts. Participating in such an activity bonded my team in unexpected ways. It allowed us to feel the gratification of mattering and allowed serious conversations about values and the importance of sharing. If you were looking for a teaming building exercise, there is nothing coming close to this one!

To be brutally honest, the Christmas' gifts operation serves its purpose. The initiative pleases the stakeholders. We could have stopped there, after all, we are forever part of being the good guys! But this wasn't about public relations nor about image, it was about the children!

In essence, gestures like that are tools that can raise awareness to a much more profound problem that needs to be addressed at its core foundation. Then the gifts' problem will disappear on its own, and this would only be the start.

I am not hoping, I am not dreaming. I am doing and keep pushing. That's how I pushed my new found friend, Dr. Bak into my vortex.

This is **AFTERMATH - BUSINESS AFTER THE GREAT PAUSE.**

In time of crisis,
It is the perfect opportunity
To reinvent who we are.
Dr. BAK NGUYEN

CHAPTER 3

"THE SHIELD"

by Dr. BAK NGUYEN

We are corporate people, ambition is our core. We have the mean to shape the word with our ideas, productions, solutions and distributions. We all understand the risks and rewards of being in business.

After a successful launch, once we've reached the corporate level, success is often coming with the size of the investments. I will borrow the word of Gordon Gekko here:

"Greed, in the lack of a better word, is good."
Oliver Stones

We have to evolve and to adapt. We all have. Most of us are much better than the average on that aspect since that's how we have survived our crisis and eventually rose. But this time, it's **REBOOTING TIME**, no stone will be left unturned. I hope that you've realized that by now.

People can criticize us as much as they want, they still need us. We are the producers of society, inventing, providing and distributing the needed goods, tools and leverage. The more we are connected with our markets, the bigger our market shares.

This is how Steve Jobs successfully brought back Apple from the blink of bankruptcy, by empowering the dreamer within each of us. That's also how Google became the internet while it was a latecomer into the game, by democratizing the information. That's how Facebook became an empire, by empowering our need to display and to matter, or our need for voyeurism.

Even Starbucks succeeded in connecting with our need to indulge ourselves with comfort. Haven't you ever asked yourself why are you paying $6 for a coffee and accepting the intake of so many calories, in this trend of banning fast food? Well, because they've created a genuine connection with their customers.

All those companies succeeded because they have successfully created an emotional bond with their customers and fan base. What are you doing to rival with them? Because yes, now that everything has been shut down, you are competing with them for the interests of the public and the attention of the governments.

Using the experience of my own industry (dental), we didn't stand a chance while, as an essential needs for society, we were put in the balance with the Cirque du Soleil. Both a struggling, one is an industry, the other, a symbol. Guess who had the ear of the government and the favor of the public when it came for a buying out?

To embrace the **REBOOT** to upgrade our values and social impact is not only good, it is out of greed. We are Gordon Gekko's pals, and we do not have to excuse ourselves for it. We are the people bearing the evolution of the world on our shoulders, we and our teams.

So if it takes **GREED** to get us out of this mess, it is surely a much better alternative than to embrace **FEAR**! At least, with **GREED**, democracy, freedom and individual rights will be preserved.

In the experience of Dr. Lacoste, trying to help the Haitian people, how did he react when he saw people selling what he gave them the day before? He told me that a woman even tried to sell him one of his toothbrushes! Well, he doubled down and pushed his team to do even more. Between eating and brushing, he made his peace.

With this in mind, we are we, corporate leaders. If what drive us are our ambitions and greed, fine, but at least let have some good out of this!

To restructure our societies and corporation with a philanthropic core at its center is a much better deal than the marketing and public relations campaign we could engage into. The outcome is far more significant, especially if that will help all of us back on track at the end of confinement.

We might even have a shot at the biggest expansion of our organization in the midst of the worst recession of our time. And what if the recession is not as bad as mentioned?

It would be thanks to leaders like you keeping their employees at work and lending a hand to the community. Do that and what government officials will dare shut you down or refuse you the needed grant?

"Stay in the shadow and suffer the consequence of being left in line and being denied, forgotten."
Dr. Bak Nguyen

The philanthropic component is not only a shield but your best leverage ahead. More than providing your organization with the needed immediate attention, from both the public and the governments, it will save you millions if not tens of million in marketing and PR.

How much? This will be left for interpretation, but if you want a guideline, here it is. Brokerage fees are often accepted at 5%. Marketing usually ranks more between 10-20%. Well, we will still need marketing. How about 2%, isn't that a fair deal, a good one? 2%

in money, and 5% in time. I came to that number looking into the resources that, as a company, we are now spending to recruit and maintain good people. Well, that 5% in time can be given as mentorship to inspire and prepare what will eventually be the future of our organization. Win-win, no?

Laid like this, the public and naysayers will then criticize us about leveraging, in our favor, the needs of others. But if we stop pointing fingers and drop the hypocrisy, we are doing a great service to society as a whole while keeping our effort sustainable, since it is now part of our inner core.

"Let GREED be the force for change, good and sustainable change. GREED will make it last and will spread it throughout the world."
Dr. Bak Nguyen

Just like you, I have no interest in endless talks and hypothetical solutions. I have no time to waste. This is a sounded logic and wise financial decision. But by the end of it, everyone will be out of this one with a win.

That's what I meant when I felt shame listening to leaders like Dr. Lacoste telling me from the passion of his heart, what he's done. It is the same feeling that pushed me to commit myself to contribute my influence while I already had so much on my shoulders.

What would I usually do? To write him a check and to resume my life. He will be pretty happy to receive that check and genuinely grateful. Until he calls me back next year, and the year after… until I start avoiding his calls. That's written in the skies.

Well, in this time of crisis, the needs a bigger than ever, and who will be writing the checks? Who are avoiding the calls? Who will find the courage to pick the phone and to keep calling? The people on the ground have enough to do helping those in need, they don't need the extra burden of begging for resources.

And we, as corporate leaders and drivers of industries, when we will have the time to hear them out and to return their calls, it will be too little too late.

This makes perfect sense from all angles. Embrace **PHILANTHROPY** as a **corporate shield** to insure your relevancy and popularity. Use that shield to expand your market in the worse recession of modern times and rewrite History before it is even written!

We will win the siege against the virus. Let's use our **GREED** to pull the rug under **FEAR'S** feet. We can do all of it gaining market shares, saving on marketing and PR cost and gain nobility, all of it while in auto-pilot!

"As the best defence is offence, the most powerful strengths are kindness, generosity and flexibility."
Dr. Bak Nguyen

This is what we will be asking the governments, the investors, the banks and the public as we will be addressing them for grants, loans or favors. Do so in a way that they can't say no.

Is this philosophy or finance? This would have been a question before **THE VIRUS**. Now it is **SOCIO-LEVERAGING** a core part of the new world economic order.

"Philanthropy is not just your shield,
but also your best leverage."
Dr. Bak Nguyen

Haven't you notice that Bill Gates is more popular now than ever before? Why? Because he is in philanthropy, not waiting in line nor asking for permission. Elon Musk, what do you think of him? He was leading the world green energy. He was a leader then, and in times of need, he is playing his part before we even have to ask.

Those are people usually making the headlines for the richest or next richest man of the planet. Today, they are making more than headlines, they are signing our collective imagination with permanent ink.

Trust me, they won't have to spend much more in marketing or PR in the future. And I am sure, their fortune will outgrow their current status, even on auto-pilot.

Isn't that the dream of every corporation, of any leaders, to matter and to be loved?

"Yes, we can have it all!"
Dr. Bak Nguyen

This is the information age, the rise of the millennials and the reign of social media.

This is **AFTERMATH - BUSINESS AFTER THE GREAT PAUSE.**

In time of crisis,
It is the perfect opportunity
To reinvent who we are.
Dr. BAK NGUYEN

CHAPTER 4

"WE ALL SMILE IN THE SAME LANGUAGE"

by Dr. ERIC LACOSTE

The idea that a child is heading straight to full mouth dentures at 20 years old disgusts me. There are no excuses for that in a country like mine, Canada, regardless of their social-economic status.

In Haiti, I did the best I could with my experience and the means at our disposal. Mine were time and passion. At home, I had to do much more, I had more experience and incomparable means.

I studied the failures of our systems and decided to provide free dental care to children (cares not covered by the universal Quebec health insurance). Many passionate colleagues before me fought to change this non-sense. They are still waiting for a win. I simply did not want to join this wait.

I wanted to be an agent of immediate positive change; I wanted to circumvent as much resistance as possible to generate tangible results, and by doing so, I had a chance at setting an example and got people to buy in, rather than fighting bureaucracy that most likely would see expenses where I see investment in the community.

So I found a way to get sponsored in part, to get discounts in other parts, to get all the toothbrushes we needed. Sadly the number of electric toothbrushes are insufficient for the number of children we see, so we had to set up criteria's to figure who would benefit the most of what type toothbrush.

Our established protocol mandates that everyone receives personalized instructions just like I did with my own children at a very young age. Thanks to other initiatives that will explain later, I was able to enlist the collaboration of colleagues to provide required treatments outside of our own expertise. The system works beautifully, and we are able to provide quality care to a fair number of children.

This part of our mission is clear: to promote dental health, to contribute to a healthy mouth and a beautiful smile through prevention and treatment. Again we could have stopped there. Once the dental objectives reached, we were not only the good guys but the really good guys. But in truth, something else came.

Spending time with those kids, you get to know them, and you get to know their story. Because of their unique way to communicate with you, once they trust you, you establish a bond. I am pretty good at that, and so it unfolds.

I stood helpless to see my kids suffer as collaterals of a divorce that I couldn't stop, it became part of my DNA to do all I could to alleviate the suffering of my own children and of any other children on my path.

Maybe my heart is too soft, or more possibly I believe that we, as humans, should do much more to protect our children around the globe. A better future starts with them. That is obvious, and yet, so often ignored.

To better illustrate what I am trying to say, I will provide examples presenting slight modifications to fully protect the identity of these kids but those stories are true and all verifiable.

Amy, aged 11, was looking at my multiple diplomas hanging on the wall. She looked puzzled and said:

- This is a lot of work.
- Yes, I answered, it surely is.
- I would like to become an architect, but I can't!
- Why?

It was my turn to be puzzled. She went on to explain that she had two half-brothers and it was her responsibility to take care of them in the evening, so she could never do homework.

If this had been Hollywood, I would have stolen the scene of Will Smith's movie the **Pursuit of Happiness** when he explained to his son to never let anyone tell him he could not do something..."If you have a dream you have to protect it."

In reality, this is Laval, Quebec, not Hollywood, it was now my problem, my responsibility to find a way. I suited up and started a new mission, my quest. Yes, I had all the capabilities to tutor her, but young Amy needed a role model, a successful woman she could relate to that could not only tutor her but also share experiences. She needed a mentor.

We eventually found her the right mentor. Caroline, a university student, would pick her up from school twice a week, bring her a snack, head to the library to work, chit chat and bring her home. We paid Caroline and took care of all the expenses.

Could Caroline have volunteered? Maybe, but her reality as a student herself, she needed money, and as the stronger link in the equation, I had the means thus creating a full circle balance where everyone benefits and contributes.

"Sometimes, dreams need a little help."
Dr. Eric Lacoste

The expert social worker made sure that Amy's mom would be on board and that the family dynamic would adjust accordingly. For Amy, a new chapter bearing hopes and opportunities began.

I would check-in from time to time. Through the social worker, Amy could reach me if she feels the need. At the end of the day, my word is my honor.

David benefited from another part of our program before I actually met him. He loved boxing. We paid for his classes and equipment. When he came to me, he told me all about his training and the benefits.

"Basically, it was boxing or the XBOX and chips…"
Dr. Eric Lacoste

David's teeth were horrible. He needed approximately 8 to 10 thousands in dental cares. Luxury? Not when you are almost 15 and that you will soon go to summer job interviews. It just had to be done, period.

Every time we won and made something happen, we felt empowered, but every time it did not work, we felt like we lost badly, just like in playoff game in professional sports. A part of me could relate to

David's story. As sports have always been a big part of my life, from my years in Tae Kwon do to my years with Laval University's Rouge et Or, as well as my bachelor in kinesiology.

Sport is an amazing teacher to so many aspects of life. Today I coach two of my son's hockey teams. I do so with the same spirit of mind. To have fun learning while building a positive foundation.

Experts all agree: sport can help you stay in school, keep you away from troubles of all kinds, including drugs and prevent common health problems such as high blood pressure, diabetes and ADHD.

In recent years, playing outdoors or practicing sports lost much ground in our scholar system in favor of other disciplines. Since **THE VIRUS,** kids are playing more outside in my neighbourhood!

I could go on and on with touching stories, but the same questions would remain: can we, as a society, do better? If so, who should do what, the government, the corporations?

While I always wondered there is no better time than the **THE GREAT PAUSE** to truly reflect on these questions, to reach out to others with the hope of creating a new economic model, a new social deal. A model of sustainability, of human dignity, where collaboration have a true meaning.

I strongly believe that such model can exist in harmony with a financial interest. Furthermore, I believe that it's the way for our future to thrive not just survive. We can no longer ignore the loud signals around us.

More than the magic of Christmas and the beautiful smiles, we now realized that we could not hope for any real success if we do not promote a global approach that included health, sport, arts, social and cognitive skills etc.

Our model had to evolve yet again. By no means do we have the competency to accomplish this alone. But I do have the will to find a way.

This is **AFTERMATH - BUSINESS AFTER THE GREAT PAUSE.**

In time of crisis.
It is the perfect opportunity
To reinvent who we are.
Dr. BAK NGUYEN

CHAPTER 5
"TOO BIG TO FAIL?"
by Dr. BAK NGUYEN

Somewhere in time, we were all fearful for our survival, as entrepreneurs. Those were the exciting times, the beginning, the expansions, the innovations. As we rose through challenges and adapted, we made our names and established our brand.

More than the brand, the distribution channels in place are what keep our bloodlines intact. What was our bargaining chip until now? The jobs we provide. That's how, when needed, we got the attention of the local and national officials, with the number of jobs we provide.

Well, that era has come to an end. Before this crisis, the leverage was reversed, our societies were in full employment, and we were fighting to recruit due to the demographic of our workforce (baby boomers) getting older with fewer and fewer people to replace them. Before, we were talking about finding the right people. Lately, we were just happy to find people!

There is a whole new industry flourishing from this circumstance, the headhunting business! Sure this recession will change that math for a little while, but since the demography hasn't changed much (unless we lose the fight against **THE VIRUS**), the workforce will simply change from one enterprise to another, from one industry to another. Sooner or later, we will be back fighting to recruit.

In this situation, we've lost all leverage to negotiate, unless we were part of the imagination and culture of the people. I told you that my industry (dental) represent 20-25K people in the province and about 110-150K people across the country with the assumption that for each dentist, there are 5-6 other people (assistant, secretary, hygienist, auxiliary) caring for the patient.

This is at least 100K families across Canada and 20K within my province. And yet, as we have a hard time reaching the central power.

The CIRCLE DU SOLEIL which is a local brand but now, a private enterprise mainly owned by foreign interests, who is providing a fraction of the number of jobs, most of them, not even on national soil, is having the national attention. Facts, those are verifiable facts. What does that tell you? To connect emotionally is good PR. Not just lobbying.

Even if lobbying gets you to the door, without leverage, you won't get much out of the meeting. Connect emotionally with your base, and you won't have to fight as hard for your voice to be heard.

Even if the shift of demography was in our favor, how many people are we employing? How many people are we serving? Whatever your numbers, common business sense will say that for each staff member we are employing, we are serving 100 even 1000, 10 000 customers. Our leverage is 100:1 in the worst-case scenario.

Our leverage is within our clientele, not our staff. Our staff and workforce are assets and people we cherish and have invested in, but they can't be our shield, not anymore. Just like our distribution channel, we depend on them and without them we can't operate, but when it comes to negotiating with the governments, they can't serve as leverage.

And to say that we are doing a great job servicing the population, how that works? The dental industry is servicing the nation. If you count that each dentist will see about 1000 patients a year, that's 21-22 million people a year throughout the country. Even with those numbers, we were left behind.

Sure, the industry will not disappear and will find a way back, but through hard times and investing millions in lobbying, lawsuit and representation. Doing so, we might have what we need, but much later, will have spent considerable resources and, if anything, we would have damaged even more our public persona (nobody like those complaining and claiming on the public place). This is a vicious circle and a PR nightmare!

"Nowadays, it isn't about justice, but perception. That's a new and sad reality."
Dr. Bak Nguyen

Times have changed, and so should we. We thought that we were too big to fail? Well, think again.

Within this crisis, a few names are surfacing. Bill Gates is appearing as a wise man, a visionary and leader that saw the virus coming. Elon Musk is surfacing where we didn't expect, pushing his engineers and factories to produce ventilators and giving them to the authorities.

Even Dyson is joining the war effort, converting his factories too. Google is pledging 800 million, Giorgio Armani donates 2 million euros, all in the effort of either fight the virus or to support the Economy. I am naming them, but so many more have stepped up to.

In contrast, I would like to point out a misfire in public perception. The richest man on the planet created a fund of 25 million to support his employees in these desperate times. It was announced on the Amazon website, and there was an option for the public to contribute with a donation.

It immediately backfired, the titles were reading as such: Jeff Bezos, the richest man on the planet is asking you to contribute for his employees. A few days later, M. Bezos announced the donation of 100 million to food banks. Some said too little too late, but too late for sure!

I told you that we are living in the information age, but people aren't looking for the truth, they are looking for sensation, now more than ever. In this time of age, anyone with a smartphone and a connection has the chance to beat a multi-million dollar PR campaign! Unless, you were a symbol in their imagination, a good guy, to borrow Dr. Lacoste's expression.

I don't know about you, but I am upset for Jeff Bezos. He managed to take care of his employees with 25 million and yet, what we are hearing his that he is asking for our money, with an enterprise that will flourish from this crisis. A few words have outweighed the millions.

Then, he gave 100 million, this is by far one of the biggest donations, but yet, I am not sure that he will erase the stain of the previous title. Whatever he is doing now, fixing his public persona, will have to outwork and outspend everyone else, even if he already did!

This is not good leverage, it isn't even leverage...

"Be proactive will serve you. Being reactive will cost you much more for lesser results."
Dr. Bak Nguyen

I will say it in here, thank you M. Bezos for your generosity. Any of us in your shoes will feel the frustration and anger. Connect with your base and paint their imagination with permanent ink! Philanthropy is a great deal, now that you can see the leverage and the alternatives.

No one is safe from these kinds of attacks, but the Cirque du Soleil... I am even sure that now, it will take much to even put a dent in the shine of Elon Musk.

Just like gladiators at the center of the Coliseum, once there, only the best will survive, but the victor is the one loved by the crowd! Are you loved by the crowd?

I am no consultant or PR fixer. I am someone that share your shoes and is looking to navigate these troubled times. From the beginning of this crisis, I saw the dark future and the global recession in the aftermath of the virus.

For the first time in our lifetime, all interests are aligned. With that, I saw the crisis of my industry and the voids. I raised my voice with the hope to unite everyone not engage in the frontline against the virus to prepare the next waves: **fear** and the **recession**.

Doing so, I pledge to share everything, my thoughts and my competitive edge. I understood that the day a wise friend told in an interview that the only way for all of us to get out of this crisis without amputation is that everyone keeps all their employees.

Well, that has shifted the wind completely. The wind of competition is over. Now is the time to share our competitive edge and to move forward as one. There is no good in arriving first if there is no one at the end to share our victory with.

If the world richest man is not too big to fail, no one is. This is the information age, the rise of the millennials and the reign of social media.

In time of crisis,
It is the perfect opportunity
To reinvent who we are.
Dr. BAK NGUYEN

CHAPTER 6

"YOU CAN'T GO TO WAR
IF YOU CAN'T FINANCE IT."

by Dr. ERIC LACOSTE

As time went on, I realized more and more that if I was going to do anything really worth doing, it would have to be more than what I had done up to that point.

Health is complex, and it includes all physical, mental and social. To meet the demands of my constantly evolving mission, I would need the money and ideally lots of it.

MY PARADOX

At this point in the book, I may appear to you like a social activist with a big heart who happens to be a periodontist. It is a side of me, to genuinely care.

I believe that with wealth and power come more responsibilities. I believe that when one benefits from the planet's resources, ones has to give back not only from a moral standpoint but more importantly, for the equilibrium of things.

To piggyback a ride on Dr. Bak's examples, I believe remarkable individuals such as Bill Gates and Elon Musk understood these principles, but I also believe that you do not need to be as big as them to get involved.

"In order not to perish in the long run, there must be a balance."
Dr. Eric Lacoste

Balance prevents chaos and promotes sustainability. In this day and age, examples of that are more present than ever before in History. The object here is not to make such analysis but between climate change, wars and terrorism and now **THE VIRUS** the examples a numerous.

I am not only a lion heart activist. In 2002, I went to the bank with a personalized version of the business plan that my accountant wrote. He was a respected accountant servicing the dental industry, so the numbers he presented were right, but it simply wasn't doing justice to my vision. His version had no color, no emotions, and no real message, and so I wrote my own.

Thanks to my parents, who supported me, I had negligible student loans. On the other hand, I had no serious money either. I went in and asked for 1,2 million dollars in financing to open what was, at the time, the first multi dental specialists in Quebec and probably Canada, but we did no verification to that effect.

1.2 million may be pocket change in the corporate world, but from where I came from, it was a crazy and bold ask. To get it, I had to put both my parent's and my aunt houses in guarantee! I was all in. I was backed against the wall, I couldn't afford to fail. That how I came to rehearse my signature phrase:

"I find a way."
Dr. Eric Lacoste

At the time, typical loans for a clinic were less than 500K, so by all current metrics, I was off the charts.

It worked out, or you won't not be reading this today. I started with no patients, and to this day, I still remember the first's 4 who came through my doors over a period two weeks. Why? Because the first 3 needed no treatments. After paying their consultation fees, I was still very far from making my first loan repayment.

The fourth patient needed treatment! So he became my first real patient, but after I provided all the explanation on his case, he chose the option that did not require my services! Since day one, I have always been totally honest and transparent with my patients and will remain so until I die. At that pace, I wouldn't be in business for very long…

NO PROFITS, NO BUSINESS

As my story went on, the clinic grew, and so did my career, I made money and started to enjoy the benefits. My entrepreneurial side pushed me in real estate and a few other ventures, some good, others terrible.

I made new friends along the way some much smarter businessman than myself. I have always admired successful entrepreneurs and always try to learn as much as possible from them for my own benefits.

In my wildest dreams, someone powerful would discover me and ask me to become his CEO, yeah right! But some people do win the lottery!

When I first started to think about what I would become in life, I thought of climbing the ladders of the corporate world. I shared my dream with my father, who explained to me why it would never work and why I was going to study science, not business!

I was not ready, I was too young, and I had not yet seen the **Pursuit of Happiness** yet. In all fairness to them, they wanted to protect me the way they knew how. The hierarchy of the corporate world wasn't the way to achieve that.

I stayed in school for a very long time accumulating a bachelor, two masters and a doctorate.

The MBA

No one challenged me when I decided to do an executive MBA. After all, I was running a business and maybe I just wanted to learn more about it. Not at all.

Since day one, I had a clear idea about how I would run my clinic. It just came naturally to me. I completed a MBA for two reasons and a fantasy.

First, I had to somehow learn the corporate language if I was going to speak with them at some point. Secondly, it was a great laboratory to test the ideas running in my head.

The fantasy, well you can guess, what if I meet that one person who could help me to become a corporate CEO.

PUTTING IT ALL TOGETHER

Just as I never could cross that line where you sell to a patient a treatment that he does not really need, I could never make a profit if it costs me morally. Is this why I am not running a multimillion-dollar company? I don't know. I like profit, and as I said, I like some of the finer things in life. But I also genuinely care for others.

FINANCING

To move on to the next level, I would need financing and the more, the better. Since I was about to solicit all of my stakeholders, I wanted to avoid the risk of alienating them. To accomplish that, I would need to create events that would be win-win, or they would sooner or later start dodging my calls.

In other words, cool events that people were interested in at the lowest possible cost to generate the most revenues. This was no easy task, but with time, I became very creative and quite knowledgeable in even planning. From meeting and greeting with Olympic Champion Bruny Surin, comedy show stars like Rachid Badouri, cooking lessons with speciality chefs or conferences with key business people.

This type of project is fun, quite challenging but requires going back to square one every time. This is very demanding on my organization, and the results are not necessarily predictable. I had to move to another level, talk with governments, change fiscal rules, and convince bigger corporations to join my initiative. I had to find a way.

"Success consists of going from failure to failure without loss of enthusiasm"
Sir Winston Churchill

THE VIRUS THE DISRUPTER OF EVERYTHING

March 16th, 2020, I could not go to work. In an instant, I lost most of my means to generate revenues to support my own and of course, all of my means to support the underprivileged children of my community. By now, you should expect me to say that I would find a way...

I reached out to presidents and high executives from other foundations and most were already feeling the effect of **COVID** even if we were only the beginning of the crisis! Organizations supporting health care and philanthropic work. It was self-evident that they started to loose private donors as well as corporate donors.

I heard over and over "People losing their jobs will pay mortgage and food first while companies fighting for their survival will have other concerns."

Already, conservative predictions were numbered between 15 and 30% in drop of donations, still not knowing what would be the devastating effect of an upcoming feared recession or global depression.

Listening to philanthropists and trying to find applicable solutions to my small organizations, I remembered my time in the military. The military is all about managing chaos.

In 1990, I went to the Royal Military College in St-Jean Quebec. The first thing I learned is that my leadership style was not a good fit with the military. The second thing I learned though was that discipline had the power to get you through chaos. If you could maintain structured, even under extreme circumstances, your chances for survival post-crisis were much better. Elite troupes master those principles to extremely high levels.

"If you are going through hell, keep going"
Sir Winston Churchill

THE PERFECT STORM

3 weeks in this crisis, chaos was definitely present. No income, no hope of possible resolution in sight for the near future, despite debates on chloroquine and no serious call to action. I had been through other storms before. I knew that keeping composure was essential.

I went back to the very basic thing that would keep me sain: Olympian's training regimen, discipline and proactive search of solutions. Soon enough, some ideas of them came around. Plan a garden for the summer, offering my services to a few selected organizations. I opened up to people from all horizons. This is when it happened.

I am not one to be superstitious, but it really seems that the law of attraction worked its magic and sent Dr. Bak Nguyen my way. We connected, and in no time, we opened to new possibilities. Right in the eye of the storm, we came up with a comprehensive strategy to find ways to save our industry, to support the most vulnerable members of our society and joined force writing this book, a new and innovative approach to the business community in the midst of rebooting itself.

By no means, I would pretend that we have all the answers. Maybe we have no good answers, but there is a genuine desire to reach out to others for the hope to initiate a movement, a vector for real positive changes.

This is **AFTERMATH - BUSINESS AFTER THE GREAT PAUSE.**

In time of crisis,
It is the perfect opportunity
To reinvent who we are.

Dr. BAK NGUYEN

CHAPTER 7

"GOOD BUSINESS SENSE"

by Dr. BAK NGUYEN

I told you by the end of my last chapter that I am no consultant nor PR fixer. I am one of you. If anything, I love the leverage and a great win. This is just common business sense to me, even sharing what I know to help you through this reboot of our economy.

While Dr. Lacoste is a kind heart taking care for people on the ground, my vocation is different. I have been taught and trained to care for systems and societies. Although, my natural, I also spent more than twenty years of my life caring for people, one person at a time. So I understand both sides of the equation.

The friend and mentor I mentioned earlier, shared me his wisdom was one of the highest-ranking officers of one of our big banks. As a financier and economist, he summarized in one sentence the fix to this crisis, a fix that will come with billions in tag price. But the alternative is much worst, much much worst.

Like many of you, I built my business from the ground up. In 2003 while Dr. Lacoste was borrowing his first million, I was turning my back on Hollywood and the possibility to have a career as a film producer. For personal reason, I decided to stay a dentist, the dream and requirement of both my parents.

Then, having too much to lose not to succeed, I borrowed nearly half a million to start my first enterprise. More than once, I was at the edge, and one false move could bankrupt all of my life's work. Yes, I am always doubling down on my successes, so I am often all-in.

I am a leader, and visionary, and lately, I discovered that I am a philosopher. I hated those lectures back in college, but you do not choose your destiny, Destiny choose you!

That's how I became a world record (to be officialized, I am simply too busy to apply, but I did walk the miles) author, writing more than 60 books within 2 years and a half. I still see patients and my company has grown into a candidate to become the next bluechip of this country.

Yes, I am juggling all of this at the same time. If anything, playing on different fields helped me build my momentum, which I transfer from one field to the next. For those of you interested in the skill, please refer to **MOMENTUM TRANSFER**, my 7th book, co-written with coach Dino Masson.

I forgot to mention that many times, I have been offered to run for office, and every time, I turned them down. A few years ago, I almost said yes as I felt the need of my country and the pain of my countrymen and women. I suited up and got prepared, but fortunately, we won, and I did not have to dive in the arena, but I was ready.

That's how I came to be trained in the art of politics and power. Leveraging is a natural skill. From my past as a failed movie producer, I also kept the art of storytelling and how to package an idea. This is where I am coming from, and I am still at risk.

My career as a dental cosmetic surgeon is well assured, my patients are coming from all over the world, and yes, I am loved and respected. Strange, considering the fact that I never fit in as a dentist. I don't like dentistry. What I crave for is to genuinely connect with people. That's the key to my success, that and the skills to never give up before completing, not a task, but an ask. I do not believe in perfection, which is the worst of lies if you ask me. I believe in harmony and satisfaction.

This is why my patients love and trust me. If within this crisis, I can lose it all, I will find a way to rebuild. For as long as I am not dead, I will rebuild. My partners know it, the banks know it and even the government are starting to understand who and what I am.

But this is not the end, not yet. Just like you, I have been given the privilege of time during the **GREAT PAUSE**, waiting for our economy to collapse. I can't stand to see the Tsunami coming and not do anything about it, especially when I have time in front of me. And time, I did not have very often in my life and line of work.

Being a CEO looking to change the world from his mind and with his hands forced me to evolve beyond comprehension. Where people see the days, I see the years, where people see an alternative, I see plans, successes and failures, way ahead. And this is when I do not have the luxury of time. Imagine now!

Everything is at stake, but I have the ideas and successfully convinced the banks to invest millions in my renewed enterprise before the crisis. As the virus is affecting all the companies, mine was in the middle of an expansion. You can imagine the stress and financial burden. Not just to meet month-end, but to salvage the expansion in its whole. This is hundreds of millions that we are talking about, hundred of millions in possible investment at stake.

It is also my life's work and the cumulation of all that I've learned: business, medicine, society, politic and philosophy. But I left out philanthropy. What I learned a few years earlier in preparation to serve my country, I left aside.

Yes, I consider myself a responsible and respected citizen as I am fighting to fix society. I am empowering my peers, but I could do more. But in my shoes, one has to choose his battles. You can't mix finance, society and philanthropy all at once. Or can you?

Aware that the only way out of this one is by standing all together, keeping all the jobs, all the enterprises, all the organizations so we can avoid **FEAR** and **ANARCHY**, what I had to do was clear. I have to do it first and then share my results.

This is how I normally proceed. This is also how I have the trust and credential preceding my reputation. But this time, it won't be enough. By the time that I am done proving my point, the **GREAT PAUSE** would be over, and it would either be too late or obsolete.

So be it. I will share with you my plans and actions as they unfold. I am trying to write and wrap this book within a week, two at the most since time is the essence here. But as I do so, I am also seeking an extraordinary meeting of my board of directors and counsel of mentors to change the core of our business and to resubmit a different business proposal to the banks and investors. And what is presented will have to be executed! That's the way it is.

Well, exchanging with Eric reminded me of the power of change an idea can have on a world. I never forgot it, I just chose my battle and decided to serve my peer dentists to reform that industry for the greater good. I got the financial world on board. The presence of my mentors on my board is proof of what I am advancing.

But, this crisis reminded me that I could do so much more. I have to do more. So writing this book, I am rewriting, in parallel, my proposal due for next Monday. Today is Saturday, and I am still in my chapters and not on my plans. With hundreds of millions at stake, what do you think that my plans will be? A copy-paste of much of this book. What I will be submitting is not a just a business proposal, but a new social an economic pact for a part of the World.

I already told you that I would require of all my partners a commitment in philanthropy as our core business way: 5% of their time and 2% of their profit. This is a very risky move, and I haven't clear it out with my board yet, at the time of this writing. But I can be very persuasive and charismatic.

This is not charity, it is good business and great leverage. At the same time, I will change the financing of my first round, from 60 million (my board convinced me to drop my demands from 100M) to now 352 million, first round. Of course, the numbers can still fluctuate and the accountants will have to verify everything, but you got the idea.

Of course, I will have to justify the need and the use of the money, but since all the plans were there, it was just a matter of multiplying the numbers of locations. The price I am paying for this is the dilution of my life's work. But time is the essence and the time is now!

"I can afford to dilute my GREED, for as long as my vision can reach fructification."
Dr. Bak Nguyen

What limited me before was the integration of the market and how fast we would have our first customer. Well, as soon as this pause is waved, my business model put me back close to where I left, with the exception that most of my competitors might be in difficulty.

I decided to see them as peers instead of competitors. So I expand the business model to include them too. I am also pushing for the industry to be more human and open. This time, they felt the pain and saw the fire. Recruitment will never be easier.

"I did not create the storm, I can still surf it."
Dr. Bak Nguyen

And I will do so trying to not leave anyone behind. Again, good business sense. This is the essence of my pitch to my investors and the banks, to my mentors and board. I will have to make my case and to prove that it will payback. It already did, the fact that you are reading my story today tells me that I am still alive and on the right track.

I may have influence and impact on a small part of the world, but together, we have all of the whole to impact. The banks and governments had never been more open to listen and to risk a new opportunity and a new way. What sounded crazy yesterday is today's proposal on the table. Why? Because complacency has left the building.

With complacency gone, **FEAR** will be stepping in soon. For some, this will be good business, but for most of us, it will make our lives so much harder. Worst, society as a whole will never be the same anymore.

As much as I love to win, I am also a fervent believer of freedom, happiness and individual rights. Well, within a few months, with the arrival of **FEAR**, most of this can be relinquished as fossils of the past.

As leaders, providers and producers of society, we can't let that happen. This is why we must all fight for the survival of our businesses. Actually, that won't be enough. We must find a way to leverage our way out of this crisis, to skip the recession and to keep all of our workforces.

For this, the governments are looking to invest in infrastructures. Be that infrastructure, that bridge between profit and community, and just like Bill Gates and Elon Musk, you will rise about the naysayers and the criticisms. Maybe not the criticisms, but for each critic, you will have an army of people coming to your help, now that they know that you are fighting for them!

I can still lose it all. So why not make the most out of it and get out of this ahead?

"The best remedy to FEAR is GREED.
So, in the lack of a better word, let's leverage our GREED for the greater good!"
Dr. Bak Nguyen

I am sharing with you my future in real-time. Hopefully, by the time you read these words, you will still have the time to act. Even after the **GREAT PAUSE**, it is always the time to act, only those who would have acted first will get the most out of this.

A crisis, like a war, is when wealth changes hands at the fastest pace. Well, in the midst of the worst crisis in modern times, with the hope to defeat **FEAR** and to keep war far at bay, ride your **GREED** so all of us could follow in peace and abundance.

"Be that infrastructure, that bridge between profit and community."
Dr. Bak Nguyen

This is the information age, the rise of the millennials and the reign of social media.

This is **AFTERMATH - BUSINESS AFTER THE GREAT PAUSE.**

In time of crisis.
It is the perfect opportunity
To reinvent who we are.
Dr. BAK NGUYEN

CHAPTER 8

"A SUSTAINABLE APPROACH TO BUSINESS AND SOCIETY"

by Dr. ERIC LACOSTE

Without any intent, I convinced Dr. Bak to present to his board a target of allocating 5% of their time and invest 2% of their profit back in the community. Imagine if I really had tried!

Seriously, at no point in time, did I solicit him for such commitment. I simply explained my vision. A vision I started to develop learning in school and later acquiring experiences in the field. I think it just made simple and perfect sense to him, and so he quickly saw the benefits but also an important ingredient that would positively affect his own chances of survival post-**VIRUS**. But where does it all make so much sense?

In the book Business and Society, Archie Carroll defined the term corporate social responsibility as follow:

"The social responsibility of business encompasses the economic, legal, ethical and discretionary (philanthropic) expectations that society has of organizations at a given point in time."

Paring this definition with everything that remains post-**VIRUS** precipitated questions that were already in the air but that are now hitting us like an ice storm. The economy is in turmoil and is trying to legally adapt to the new rules.

Ethic is taking a new forefront, and I believe that philanthropy is undergoing a metamorphosis. By taking care of each other, we can create bidirectional rapports that will uplift society, sustain at the same time, greed and profit while simultaneously uprising those who traditionally have the role of beneficiaries.

With this in mind, we can aspire to a better society and a balance that will empower us to be better prepared for other challenging moments. There is no better time for a change in paradox on how we have been doing things to this point in the History of humanity.

It's started with an idea, a book, by a group of individuals pushing for a change. To me, no one better explains this that success author Simon Sinek in his book **START WITH WHY**. As he well describes the why means why we exist? Why do we do what we do as a society? What is our purpose?

Profit is not a purpose, but a result. Our objectives why should be clear and simple: to create a better society, a more profitable one for everyone and a more balanced one so that we are collectively better prepared to face viruses and recession as one.

True leaders don't hesitate to sacrifice what is theirs for what is ours. This is not incompatible with profit. My new found friend Dr. Bak shares this vision, he empowered it with all of his might and influence.

Going back to my story, here are to me the clear benefits I found in investing in my community and what we can achieve as one on a the planetary scale, if we make it our why:

1. Active contribution to the well-being of the community.
2. Participation in the economic development of the region. By giving an opportunity to children to have a better future, we contribute to the development

of the workforce and the next generation of consumers.

3. Opportunity to support a cause that has special significance to us, personally.

4. Development of the human aspect of the corporate culture, which in turn, will contribute to our reputation and deployment of our brand image and identity.

5. The creation of powerful motivational missions for your team members who show a desire for innovation and productivity.

6. Publicity we cannot buy, thus improving our relationship with our staff, suppliers, customers and other stakeholders such as professional order in my case.

7. A privileged opportunity to share our knowhow and expertise to non-profit organizations that can benefit from expertise they can't always afford.

I have personally experienced and measured all those benefits in my own enterprise. True entrepreneurs are focused on more than the bottom line of their financial statement. They find a way to contribute to society, and they lead the way in seeking innovative solutions to both financial and social issues. So will the real entrepreneurs rise up at the time were humankind need it the most?

I have said it before; I do not pretend to have all the answers. This is much larger than me. But a simple conversation with Dr. Bak started a cascade, this cascade. If a simple conversation can lead to changes like this, imagine how it would be if the whole planet resonates to the same beat?

This is **AFTERMATH - BUSINESS AFTER THE GREAT PAUSE.**

In time of crisis,
It is the perfect opportunity
To reinvent who we are.
Dr. BAK NGUYEN

CHAPTER 9

"PHILANTHROPY IS NO CHARITY"

by Dr. BAK NGUYEN

Now that we all agreed that philanthropy is good leverage, both social and financial, let's dig into the hows. The cool part here is that one can be as creative as he/she desires. But since time is the essence, here a few suggestions:

In my proposal to my partners, 5% in time and 2% in money, here what I encourage:

TIME

Usually, a person will work about 8 hours a day. 30 to 40 hours a week. For the math in here, we will consider 40 as a norm. Assuming that people have 4 weeks off a year, that breaks it down to 2 hours a week of voluntary work. What is 2 hours a week? Seriously?

That time can be spent on:

VOLUNTARY EXPERTISE

Using their own expertise to help/care for the least fortunate in our community. In other words, keep doing what they do best. If you are scared of cannibalizing your clientele by giving our expertise for free while charging the others, you can keep charging the same to everyone and then, pay someone else to do that 2 hours of voluntary work. But with that protection, where is the leverage?

FIELD IMMERSION

You can have your people to actually go out and help on the field, helping actively the organizations. This will require more organization, but it can be a wonderful team-building exercise. If you are willing to have a coordinator, you could build the perfect PR campaign while doing some real good on the field.

The problem is that you do not want to be too far from your core expertise since you are not a voluntary workforce, but a corporate citizen with added value. If you want my advice, never leave your expertise behind. That's your best business card, even if that wasn't the main purpose of the exercise.

MENTORING

You can also stay closer to your own field, lending a hand to the schools and universities offering internships and closely monitor a 1 on 1 relation between your staff and an apprentice. This is no cheap labor, that 2 hours will have to be to the benefit of the mentoree if you want any social leverage out of this one.

The exercise cannot be seen as a recruitment operation, so you must go out of your way to really share experiences and useful information to help the youth and next generation.

If you were looking for the competitive edge, the youth talks and shares much more than the average population. Give them a reason to brag about their experience in your ranks, and you will have the best PR campaign ever!

Do not forget that around each person, there are many people. By the end of the day, this will be a great PR, recruitment and marketing campaign. It also has the effect to elevate your staff will socio empowerment, a mentor will always stand taller than an employee!

VOLUNTARY MARKETING

Another way to go around is to push for a new way to distribute your service, online, for example. Well, have a specific service offer to the entire population for free. That's also giving back.

This practice will gain you much more favor from your own clientele, but can easily be perceived as great marketing rather than philanthropy. Between you and I, it is serving the community, and if we include our giving back to those keeping us in business, why not? If by the end of the day, you are doing more business, you will have more profit to share! It's still a win-win situation.

You see, the problem with philanthropy and social work is that people are looking to be perfect and above criticisms. You and I know that no matter your actions and decisions, some people will always criticize. And don't even ask those people what they are doing for the community and society! Within days, Saint Bill Gates had his name tarnished now that he advocates for universal vaccination. Let the talker talk, we have miles to walk!

Find your way to make it work, and for as long as you are comfortable with the implementation and the finance, you will keep it going. This cannot be an effort forcing you and your team to go way out of your comfort zone.

"Better a smaller change that will last than a good deed that will fade."
Dr. Bak Nguyen

So stay away from the experts and those telling what to do. Look around and find something that will make your team and you feel good at the end of EACH day, not just one day.

TEAMING UP ANOTHER INDUSTRY

This one can be tricky. This is inter-industry's diplomacy. Lend your expertise to another friendly industry and share. This will strengthen the DNA of both organizations as you are exchanging skill, ideas and management style.

Your staff will surely appreciate the break from the routine and the novelty of ideas and new perspectives. This is only step one, since the community will need to gain something out of this too.

Until now, you were giving back looking at your our expertise, your own bellybutton. It was a great value to the community and exceptional marketing, but you did not have the chance to reinvent yourself, safely. Joining with another industry will take care of the reinventing.

This is the paradox of today's society. We want people to be open and to share, but as it comes to delivering, we want experts, tunnelled vision on what they do best, the only thing they can do. Well, teaming up with another industry to have a social impact will brand you as open while keeping your expertise in place.

You will still need to negotiate with the other party a common cause and the logistic of the partnership. I told you, this one is trickier. But as usual, more risks, more gains!

Whatever you decide, for as long as you feel good about it, you are winning. With minds like ours, this is barely step one. Soon enough, you will understand the new dynamic and find ways to leverage and improve the efficiency of your process, thus augmenting your impact on the community.

And how to finance this? Well, look into your current budget, what are you spending in team building, in continuous education, in PR, in marketing. Derive part of that budget to your new philanthropy department and test. Test and readjust. Actually, test and have fun!

The effort does not have to be all yours, involve your team in the decision process, so they too, can contribute and donate. As soon as they feel genuine connection and empowerment, they might surprise you with the result.

By sitting down with them, you are leading the way, but you are also sending the message that they matter and that you are partnering up with whoever wants to step up. Your human resource directors will tell you how beneficial this can be. But usually, do we risk such exercise in our business unit?

Philanthropy is your excuse to run your social lab test. This is how Zappos started and rose to the top. Have fun and experiment.

In my own experience, as I connected periodically with my staff in confinement, one of my team members, Farah Saucedo, a finance officer at **Mdex & Co**, rose in social implication. On her own, she took the initiative to help people in need in the local community. She called for people to donate and for people in need to reach out.

Within 2 weeks, she helped 164 families. When I learned about her initiative, I had tears of joy, tears that I hid behind my smile. I empowered her at my best, giving her the influence and socio leverage that I have. I interviewed her on my podcast and spread of the challenge for people to give away clothing as they are looking to clean up their closet. To give it some viral power, we hash tagged it **#REBOOT**.

Even if my company was in shutdown, I also felt the need to reward and empower those taking initiatives. I put her back on the payroll as she does not need to struggle for her own survival while she was taking care of others.

She never asked for any of it. Why did I do so? Because it was good common sense! And she was proving my point: there is a way to stay relevant, even in pause!

"Philanthropy is leverage and social impact, not charity."
Dr. Bak Nguyen

MONEY

One will think that this is the easy part. Absolutely not. To ask for money is one thing, to ask for money repeatedly is something else. This is where we see the fundamental difference between philanthropy and charity.

While philanthropy is a way of life and a philosophy, charity is ego with a blessing. Twist the words as you might, sooner or later, you will come to my point.

Writing a check is charity. It will make you feel good and will do some help, but there is simply little to no leverage possible out of it. Am I evil to leverage on my actions? This is who we are and how we made it this far! Do not fall into the trap of candor, in the name of good!

Do good and leverage doing so. You will end up doing even more good, much more good. I suggest you organize your labor forces and teams around to discuss with them how the money will be distributed. Have them be part of the conversation.

If anything, your organization and its flaws will not be the main subject of the conversation for a change! Empower those rising into a leading position. Once again, you are a leader, not the sole donor, so give them a chance to contribute and to share the drive and leadership.

My advice is to have a long term plan, so you see lasting results and can have both your team and the public to follow the progression on the field.

Money is leverage. There are experts to build and to dispenses the needed services and infrastructures. Having your people at the table and giving them the chance to decide will empower them with the idea that they too, can change the world! They will love you for it and will now see you as a leader, not the boss to negotiate with. If you were looking for a human face and a way to connect with your team, this is a golden opportunity.

Have the check ready and spend the needed time to include and empower your team to be part of the solution and the leverage. Soon enough, they will want more.

We all know that to be sustainable, we need infrastructures and to run on auto-pilot, not having to go through the decision process every time. At the same time, we do not want to be committed in a cause for too long.

So no, do not write a blank check. Participate in the journey and involve your team. Just like a champion needs to feed on his/her victory, you and yours will need to feed on your social impact to grow and to keep evolving. Have a project, have the talk and share the power. There was no risk involved!

"Leadership is not to seize control but to inspire the control in others. Now, change control for empowerment."
Dr. Bak Nguyen

If you look at my career, how did I manage to be that influential while the title on my business says that I am a dentist? A few years back, I was involved in helping a medical/social cause looking for resources and solutions for the short and long terms.

I was far from my core expertise, but a friend convinced me that the cause needed my help. I went in, not knowing how I could contribute. Well, within days, I stayed true to my character but listened to their problems and suggested my angle.

A week later, we were announcing real progress on the ground. How? Because I had access to resources that they never thought of. I remember in the press conference announcing our advancement, the reporter who just interviewed me jumped out of his chair looking at my business card, reading that I was a dentist.

It was almost condescending, but he gave us the needed coverage. This is what it looked like when you are too far away from your core expertise, people like experts, people trust experts, but they still want open minds and hearts. They want, I never said that they were.

Long story short, I was encouraged by the initial success, so I push further, reaching out and looking for more resources and opportunities.

There was no money or business there, just a universal cause in need of attention and sustainable resources. I went looking for infrastructures that could serve in the long run. Within weeks, we were sitting at the table of the decision-makers.

We got our primary goal reached, save the immediate life in question. For the long term, I set up the negotiating table for two industries to collaborate and to build a sustainable and lasting solutions. To my disappointment, the negotiations did not fell through.

Later on, the leader of one of the 2 parties told me that I have advanced this cause more in a matter of weeks that it was done over the last 30 years. I took the compliment but was still very upset about the outcome. Well, I cannot blame myself, but I still had no result to show, forgetting that we just save a human life and a family.

But the experience came with an unexpected benefit. I rose in influence and confidence. What I learned was the more I was taking care of someone else's problem, I had no liability and just the possibilities to gain leverage and gain. Even if there were no material gain, I rose in influence, not waiting in line or fighting my way through.

"Taking care of other people's problem, you have leverage and no liability. This is your way to score with least resistance."
Dr. Bak Nguyen

Looking back, would I do things differently? Absolutely. I was naive and just gave without looking over my shoulder. Hey, they were the one asking for help! But in everything, there is always a game of power and control, an aftermath and politic.

I regret the failure of this initiative, especially the tens of thousands of lives that could have been save within my lifetime. To tell you the truth, I am pissed! But what do you want? I was a newbie, the underdog that no one saw coming. I didn't see that coming either. The next time, I will be ready, and still, they won't see me coming. I will be wiser.

Then, a few years later, I applied the same creativity and audacity to other battlefields. I kept growing my confidence and creativity. I gained more and more influence and power, even if my business card still say that I am just a dentist.

Is that philanthropy or the best field experience I ever had? It is my life and my story to tell. I did the deed, walk my talk, and I outgrew my own existence. That's how I later became a prolific author and an influencer, not on social media, but in more than one industry and in more than one circle of power.

Usually, I act more in society's matter, much less at an individual matter. This is just how I see leverages and angles. But when I met with Dr. Lacoste, pulling his heart and soul to help people he can name by their first name, I was moved to my core.

We need both to make this society work. We both care, we are both convinced by our mission, and we both will not give up easily. "We will find a way!"

So what is your way? How will you leverage on philanthropy to write your legacy? How will you leverage, risk-free, on the fun and novelty to reinvent yourself and rebrand your organization? I am sure, the next time we will meet, we will be reading how you change the world for the better while expanding your market shares!

> "Philanthropy was my way out from
> my own success, my own prison."
> Dr. Bak Nguyen

This is the information age, the rise of the millennials and the reign of social media.

This is **AFTERMATH - BUSINESS AFTER THE GREAT PAUSE.**

In time of crisis,
It is the perfect opportunity
To reinvent who we are.
Dr. BAK NGUYEN

CHAPTER 10

"THE PLEA"
by Dr. ERIC LACOSTE

A GENERATION IN TURMOIL

In my 17 years of practice, for countless times I had conversations with patients who were profoundly unhappy with their work, pathologically stressed with life and overwhelmed by the crazy pace imposed by society.

All too often this resulted in poor health habits, medication, alcohol or drug abuse, which, in turn, are contributing to our annihilation. Every time I had this conversation, inside of me, I thought: this needs to change because this pace is killing civilizations. Profit is good but maybe not if it's killing its manpower, destroying the environment and the planet.

Our current business models are too often designed on performance with little to no regard to the serious social issues that we can no longer choose to ignore.

Ecosystems around the globe are suffering from Australia to California, from Europe to the Amazon forest. The newest threat, **THE VIRUS**, makes absolutely no discrimination on who's who! It does not matter if you are a head of state, a CEO, form the working class or from poverty.

"You are killing yourself for a job that would replace you within a week if you dropped dead. Take care of yourself."
Jet Li

NO CLEAR ROAD AHEAD

The news on **THE VIRUS** is changing at such an alarming pace, I almost can't keep up, and I certainly can't even write fast enough.

In a matter of more or less 24 hours, industrialized countries are fighting for the new hottest commodity, the N95 mask. The prime minister of England is in intensive care, and the United States are preparing for the worst with almost 2000 dead during the last 24 hours.

Lost in a sea of press on the topic, another article raises the alarm on the fact that developing countries don't have the resources to fight this enemy effectively. They fear the worst. Haiti for example. This poor island in the Caribbean will be quite alone to fight our common enemy and will have very little political weight in the modern fight to acquire N95 masks.

The poor always finishes last. Here or abroad, that's unfair, and this has to change! We have to stand as a society, we have to be one with the planet! That's why I advocate for new ways of doing business. That's why the model of distribution of wealth should evolve to allow **GREED** and **SHARING** to walk together and to create equilibrium.

The popular rainbow, slogan in the windows, and the signs on the streets are not so encouraging anymore. If world leaders can't even coordinate together for the fight against a common enemy, how can we honestly hope that all will go well?

I said it before, I may be a periodontist, but above all, I am a health care professional, and I genuinely care for others. I hope that writing this will serve my community.

Right now, my activities are paralyzed except for a few emergencies to manage. As a general rule, my profession is on the sideline; Why? I don't know. I contacted different authorities because maybe they forgot that we are there. After all, they have so much to do.

"The biggest mistake we make in life
is thinking we have time."
Cobe Bryant

A few articles talked about the pressure felt by the government to alleviate the confinement measures. Why? Because of its impact on the economy. We really need to restart the economy in order to feed the system, the whole system. That scares me.

We are in such a hurry to go back to feeding the beast, nourishing the old model. We haven't even taken the time to think this through or ask ourselves if this model really is compatible with the future of the human race. Yet there is an urge to go back to our comfort zone and put our collective conscience back to sleep.

The planet is screaming for help, and we need to redefine our consumption habits and promote a better regionalization of the way we have been doing business.

For this to happen great minds must come together. It must be done now while we are on pause and rebooting. Productivity and growth at all costs are causing unsustainable pressure both on people and our natural resources.

We must not drown ourselves in blindly positive slogans fleeing the seriousness of the exercise, one that we desperately need to do on a global scale.

During this crisis, we should grab the opportunity to identify where we are coming from and where we want to go as a society and as one world standing together.

In light of troubled times, current economic models show that they are not too big to fail and that every time they do fail, they cause deep scars and terrible damages. We need to improve those models and to raise the bar.

WE NEED MORE LEADERS

I have said it before; I always admire my entrepreneur friends who are more successful than me. More specifically the way they are ahead of the game. The rare ability to make the right move at the right time is not given to everyone.

They are from the same bread as sports legends such as Wayne Gretzky, Tom Brady, Michael Jordan or Pélé. I have the privilege to call Olympic champion Bruny Surin a friend. I studied him. He displays those qualities that make some individual into game-changers.

An unbelievable sense of work ethic, the power to never quit and a vision that allows finding a path. In his own words: Go get it!

"Leadership is not a licence to do less;
it is a responsibility to do more."
Simon Sinek

The world needs corporate leaders to rise up and be the driving force to implement change for the greater good where economic interests and society can evolve as one. Why them? Because, they like professional athletes, they have the ability to be game-changers.

A CHANGE IN PARADIGM: THE FUTURE OF OUR PLANET DEPENDS ON IT

If by now you haven't figured out why I believe we have to invest in our children and why we should level the field to provide true opportunities to underprivileged children, I will spill it out again. The current economic model is driving us to our peril, and we can no longer ignore this.

True change can be initiated by today's leaders but should be driven by the minds of tomorrow, AKA our children. We cannot only be driven by pure profit. A new vision must give all stakeholders an equal voice while all interests are met.

"COVID -19 is a great reminder of this:
all humans are equal stakeholders in this fight."
Dr. Eric Lacoste

Change requires courage and resilience. Our children often have both. Let's teach them that change is possible by initiating a new global initiative and a better way of doing business, one significant transition at a time.

Let's put our minds together, create a new model, a better one, one compatible with creating collective wealth and where profit and greed will also support communities and help social issues. We owe it to ourselves; we owe it to our children. It's fundamental to the human species.

NEW WORLD ORDER, NEW INDUSTRIES

Public health specialist and director of the international union against tuberculosis and lung disease, Gan Quan, proposed a bold statement:

"The best thing that the tobacco industry can do in the fight against **THE VIRUS** is to immediately stop production and sale of tobacco... it is the best time to quit smoking." supporting his arguments with a preliminary Chinese study that suggested that smokers infected with **COVID** virus were more severely affected and suffered greater complications.

Now, to be clear, I will not advocate for the disappearance of an entire industry and all the consequences it could have. But what if it does happen, what if some transformations are imposed to us? We will need corporate leaders to lead the way and take the hard decisions while creating new commercial opportunities, thus transforming chaos into alternatives.

It is easy too easy to suggest to transform the culture of tobacco to favor agriculture, feed our planet with better foods and reduce the incidence of devastating disease such as cancers.

This is especially true when I have personally diagnosed oral cancer secondary to tobacco consumption several times and seen firsthand its devastating effects on the life of those patients and loved ones. However, it is not the purpose of this book. For the first time in our lifetime, all interests are aligned. Therefore, all stakeholders, from all industries should come together and find a way.

Just like in this example, some proposition may require hard and drastic changes, and cause disruptive changes in the lives of 1,2 billion smokers on the planet. It would, however, promote health, the environment and an industry conversion that could benefit to the world's population all while shifting an economy to another, not killing an economy.

To support this idea, journalist Ahmed Kouaou interviewing Serge Morand, a health ecologist and researcher who made a very strong point explaining why in is expert opinion, the **COVID** crisis is intimately caused by human activity. The facts he presented and his reasoning led him to explain that current agricultural models should be reviewed from a territorial perspective rather that from stock markets standpoint.

He further explained that the de-globalization of agriculture would promote food security; generate honest revenues for local farmers all while preserving biodiversity and health of consumers. Such ideas are game-changing events definitely but not without the creation of new sustainable opportunities.

THIS IS NOT A DREAM, THIS IS A VISION

The more I read, the more I realize that so many other experts in other fields have similar concerns: we need a change now to ensure our survival tomorrow. So I did a post on LinkedIn to test my theory.

"The more I read, the more I exchange, the more I realize that many of us are seeing the same thing: Humanity has to change now to protect its future. We have to share ideas, our vision to initiate a movement. It is with the power of corporate leaders, entrepreneurs and professionals that we have the power to influence and innovate."

It was viewed and liked 1320 times in less than 24 hours. I am not alone. In my own industry and scale, I was able to start implementing change by making basic dental care more available to children in need. All, without turning my back on profit or growth. To add significance to my various initiatives, I established different metrics to measure the effectiveness and to validate our process.

Then, I was able to influence a colleagues to join my initiative, and more recently, I influenced Dr. Bak to play a role of importance in the renewal of the dental industry, changing his own business model, while never turning his back on profitability. His work might affect a whole industry. That's a lot of people.

It all started will a vision, a hope. Imagine initiatives across the planet could resonate at the same beat. The road ahead may still not be so clear yet, but it is the power of corporate leaders and entrepreneurs across the board that we can make a better tomorrow.

This is **AFTERMATH - BUSINESS AFTER THE GREAT PAUSE.**

Dr. Eric Lacoste

In time of crisis,
It is the perfect opportunity
To reinvent who we are.
Dr. BAK NGUYEN

CHAPTER 11

"SHARING IS THE WAY TO GROW"

by Dr. BAK NGUYEN

Since I tasted philanthropy, I got addicted to its leveraging power. As I said, I grew in influence because my social impact is getting bigger and broader. To summarize that in a short sentence is: the more I care about issues affecting many individuals, the stronger I grow my confidence and thus, my influence.

You took the time and the interest to read us. By now, if you are still reading, it's because you are coming on board. I thank you for your trust. But I want to reassure you that it is not all coming from me.

I will take this chapter to show you how I came to be this way and who taught me to leverage on philosophy, society and to combine them with finance.

Dr. ROGER BOURCIER

He was my first mentor, a gentleman from the old times. He taught me how one can find true meaning and love, even from something as dry as dentistry. I saw patients with tears of joy, as they were learning that Dr. Bourcier will keep practicing for a few more years.

I saw people so afraid of going to the dentist falling asleep on his chair, under his care. Even if Roger does not talk much, you can feel the kindness in his presence. He gave me hope as I was looking for myself and my purpose in life. He also proved to me that you can find fun in everything, even in dentistry.

If I have succeeded treating people, even if I don't like dentistry, it is thanks to what I learned from Dr. Bourcier: genuine kindness and authenticity. Today, I am leading the change in my industry.

"I treat people, not teeth."
Dr. Bak Nguyen

Dr. KIEN QUAN DIEC

He is the father of 2 of my best friends and a mentor to me. From a very young age, I have always been interested in the stock markets, the options and the leverages of finance.

Back in high school, I was already initiated to the world of options and contracts. I read as much as I could find on the matter, but I didn't have any money to invest. Then, fate and destiny brought me to other horizons.Dental surgery, movie making, real estates, entrepreneurship.

It was only by the day that I became a dad and visited Dr. Diec that I was reminded of my past passion. He took the time to reinitiate me, and within days, I was trading. This was shortly after the financial meltdown of 2008. My financial advisors lost the vast majority of my portfolio, but they were not to blame, the whole market came down.

It is then that I took over, telling myself how worst could I do? Within months I perfected my trading skill and multiple my portfolio. Then, greed took over and made me overconfident. I started to take more and more risks, to the point of quadrupling my portfolio within a few months. I lost touch with reality and paid the consequences. I crashed myself. But it was unreal, within a morning I could close tens of thousands in profit. Usually, by noon, I was out of the market. Even if Dr. Diec taught me the tools, he strongly disagreed with my methods. His main teaching was:

"The stock market, just like in life, is a big buffet.
Sit down and eat as much as you need.
Then, clean your place and let someone
else enjoy their turn."
Dr. Kien Quan Diec

To this day, this is what I cherish from his teaching. After my crash, I didn't want to try to come back at the market to just recoup my losses and lost gains, this is how gamblers are operating. So I swallowed my pride and pain and moved on. Then I put all of my energy to study and learn the crisis of 2008, of the derivatives and what caused the melting down of the financial system.

He monitored me from a distance and later on, share with me how he was impressed by my discipline and composure through such loss. I just prove myself worthy of managing money, much money. It is not about the gain or the loss, but how to last it in the long terms. I also mastered most of the tools of finance.

I learned about my character and the possibilities of Life. When I said that philanthropy is leverage, well, I learned the financial leverage studying with the wise Dr. Diec.

Dr. Mohamed Benkhalifa, PhD. in political science and lawyer.

I met Dr. Benkhalifa on my dental chair. Yes, he started as my patient. Quickly, we connected, and our dental appointments became philosophical discussions.

The day I felt my calling to rise up for my country, I went to him and hired him as a political coach ad consultant. The man is a member close to the United Nations and has close to his heart the values that world organization.

He trained me in the art of international and national policy and diplomacy. He showed me the art of influence. Social leveraging, that was me, applying my knowledge of finance to the complex universe of people. I became a different kind, a different bread.

I value my independence as a thinker and the freedom of my actions as an entrepreneur. I was ready to run for office. But while I felt the need of my country, I did not necessarily have the ambition. When the battles were won and that I did not have to run, I moved on.

To this day, I am one of Dr. Benkhalifa's big regrets. Maybe one day in the future, but not for as long as my country can do without me. I still have a long journey in front of me.

From Dr. Benkhalifa, I learned the world of politics and power, of influence and society. What I kept was philanthropy, to apply leverage to society for an outcome for the greater good. From that day on, I wanted to change the world for the better.

Dr. Jean De Serres

I met Jean as I was fighting for society. He was the head of one of the parties. He is also a seasons VC in the drugs and pharmaceutical industry. We learned to respect each other on the battlefield and became good friends sharing our passion for finance and music.

Jean is a kind soul, although a sharp financier and skill manager. He gave me the confidence to believe in my visions and to share it with confidence. Although he will describe me as a gambler willing to bet the house on my next move, he is also very respectful of my vision and discipline seeing things through.

We wrote a book together, **THE RISE OF THE UNICORN**, telling the story of a start-up we shared. If there is one thing I learned with Dr. De Serres is to see beyond the means. Have your goal, even if you do not have the means, then work to obtain those means you need. He summarized it in a sentence in **THE RISE OF THE UNICORN**.

> "With 4 million, you can have a shot. With 40 million, you have a company and a way to survive your failures."
>
> **Dr. Jean De Serres**

This is how I learned to apply my leverage and tools at the society's level. I still care for my patients at an individual level, but I never looked back from there.

CHRISTIAN TRUDEAU

Fate and fortune brought us together. A veteran financier and senior manager, M. Trudeau was the head leading the digitalization of the Montreal stock market. He then moved on to a senior position in one of Canada biggest blue chips to create his own division. At the top of the stock market, the division he created was worth 18 billion!

Although his past is my future (I hope), we connected from a different value: he was intrigued and attracted by my skills and drive, but it is my kindness and generosity that sealed on friendship. He told me in confidence once:

"You judge the character of one looking on how he/she treats those under his command. "
Christian Trudeau

We also have much fun talking about finance and how to leverage a business opportunity into a bluechip. We wrote a book together on business and its management: **HUMAN FACTOR**.

It was his way to push me to grow even more to become a moral leader in the business world. If I had the flame of changing the world for the better and the leveraging skill to see it through, M. Trudeau grew the muscles and expanded my horizon into the big leagues.

ANDRE CHATELAIN

Andre is the former first vice-president of one of our big banks' organization. By the time he retired, he managed 100 billion in transactions annually.

Formally, he is Tranie's mentor, my wife's mentor. But we quickly become good friends. There aren't so many people you can discuss matters of society beyond the gossips, the fear and the criticisms.

Although a top financier, Andre is the kind and human manager giving a human side to the backbone of **Mdex & Co**. If there is one thing important to his eyes is how we treat our employees. And it does not have to interfere with profits or growing our market shares.

Through our discussions, I became sensitive enough to hear his wisdom and to wrap the loop: from ideas to market, from staff to society.

In the current **THE VIRUS** crisis, he is the one telling me that the only way to have an economy after the **GREAT PAUSE** is to keep all the jobs!

Actually, it is from that conversation that I had the idea of finding a way to keep all the jobs and all corporations running. I looked at different angles. Meeting with Dr. Lacoste reminded me of my power leveraging philanthropy. I put the need of the many with philanthropy, boosted by **GREED** and voila!

From caring genuinely for each individual with fun and kindness to leading society; I learned from each job, this is the fun side. To each our part of the buffet, I learned. To build and expand for society, through society, I learned.

To aim for the moon and bring people on board; they will follow if the destination is worth their time, I learned. To lead and leverage, once you know who you are fighting for, I learned. To leave no one behind, I heard.

Those are the wisdom I learned from these great minds, friends and mentors. This the foundations of this book.

And why am I sharing this as openly with all of you? Because I care. Because this is how leverage works, by showing you what you have to gain to come on board and to help. Because I owe it to my mentors to change the world for the better. And yes, because the World needs us to stand up, now more than ever!

I honor my mentors by honoring you. Thank you.

"Sharing is the way to grow."
Dr. Bak Nguyen

This is the information age, the rise of the millennials and the reign of social media.

This is **AFTERMATH - BUSINESS AFTER THE GREAT PAUSE.**

In time of crisis,
It is the perfect opportunity
To reinvent who we are.
Dr. BAK NGUYEN

CHAPTER 12
"INFORMAL POWER"
by Dr. ERIC LACOSTE

In the world, corporations are uniquely positioned to exert influence with their lobbying power and their investing power. They have direct and indirect influences through the jobs they provide and the resources they mobilize.

But like we all, **THE VIRUS** does not discriminate. It changes many, if not all the parameters, and like every other world organization, corporations must adapt.

It is generally accepted that Formula 1 racing is the pinnacle of motorsport. It is extremely glamourous and attracts some of the richest corporations. Jean Todt is the former head of Formula 1 Scuderia Ferrari from 2004 to 2008 before becoming the actual president of the **FIA, FÉDÉRATION INTERNATIONALE DE L'AUTOMOBILE**.

In a recent interview given to **MOTORSPORT.COM**, he did not hesitate to raise fundamentals questions that could significantly modify the face of Formula 1 post-VIRUS. He could not exclude the possibility that up to four of the racing teams could disappear. He explained that manufacturer's priorities were not to secure their participation in motor racing, their focus geared towards survival.

"We must be humble. We love motorsport, but it is not essential for society. So we must make sure that we make the proper choices and proper decisions".
Jean Todt

He sent a message of solidarity to humanity. "In each disaster, in each crisis, we have a lot of bad, but we also have some good". As president of the FIA, he proactively took many extraordinary measures to alleviate pressure on the teams and actively fight for the survival of this industry.

Both short and long terms sustainability of motorsport were at the heart of this interview.

"There are issues to address in every part of the world…. this is the time to demonstrate authority and responsibility."
Jean Todt

In short he emphasized that it was important to have strong governance at the top of the organization. Even in times of crisis, it is rare to see an industry leader ready to publicly admit that the world is facing stakes more important than those of his industry. This is a model to follow, and this is what, I hope, we will achieve.

WE ARE LIVING A UNIQUE HUMAN EXPERIENCE. NONE OF THE NORMAL PARAMETERS APPLY NOW

Like many of my colleagues, I sometimes rely on objective performance measurements tools and so-called dashboards. In times like this thought, I do not believe it is the right thing to do. Leadership and entrepreneurship are so much more than numbers. Too many variables are constantly changing, and more importantly, the mindset of most stakeholders is not where it was before **COVID**. If you fail to recognize this, you will struggle or maybe even perish.

I received the call of 2 different corporate leaders who wanted my opinion on my perception on resuming business **POST-COVID**. For confidentiality purposes, I will omit certain details, but in context, I was the client, and they were the suppliers.

As the conversation started, I had the feeling that they were hoping I would come up with mutually beneficial innovative strategies to promote their sales and my rate of treatment acceptance in what we believe will be a potentially very difficult market. That was not my message!

The possibility that we will face an economic recession is really high. For several reasons, patients will likely postpone elective treatments. Some will have lost their jobs or their insurance; others will potentially fear another wave or fear to be infected if no vaccine is found.

The inclination of industry leaders and influencers is to find new ways and strategies to reinstate trust in the economy, to stimulate spending and trust in the degree of safety of the protocols for procedures.

Again I questioned, is that really the way to go and even more importantly, if we approach this traditionally with discounts, promotions and brilliant marketing strategies? Is there a significant risk that we will miss out on deeper scars and issues that **THE VIRUS** will likely leave from a human standpoint? We are living a unique human experience, and none of the normal parameters apply.

So back at the heart of my discussion with the CEOs, my message was not orthodox and wasn't what they were expecting to hear! I simply do not believe in artificially boosting sales at least not in the health care industry. In 17 years plus of practice, I have never done it, and it's never been an issue. There is a level of ethics one must maintain, but really that wasn't the point.

Furthermore, in present time, We should not focus on getting back to the way things were, nor should we engage ourselves in a never-ending race to catch up with our loss, comparing ourselves to statistics. We should rather learn from our mistakes and work to be better. We should also embrace the new reality and take the time to understand what it would actually all mean. If we achieve that, the rest will take care of itself.

True to my **WHY**, I explained that the communities they are doing business with are suffering, not only the clients but their clients as well. I believe that right now, communities are more sensitive than ever to help its receiving. When business will resume, they will remember who did what.

I quickly meet a polite objection: "We cannot give to charity when our sales are down." Furthermore, one leader argued that they are all for creating value for their stakeholders. He defined this by making good quality products that doctors like to use, that meet end customers needs, making their lives better.

He placed a lot on emphasis on his valued proposition and how making it more accessible would encourage people to proceed with treatment. From his point of view, there was a way to create a spin-off where the message would say there was no better time to take care of yourself.

Talking to a doctor, he conveniently left the part about shareholder's returns in an effort not to presumably bore me with something, he thought, I might not find relevant. I was laughing inside or more so, was I boiling inside. I further explained that it was critical to enlarge the view of stakeholders, and that my point of view was more in line with his own that what perceived at first glance.

I am not asking you to give to charity, I am asking you to invest in the most vulnerable stakeholders of the communities in which you do business. This is a great opportunity! An opportunity to not only be industry leaders but community leaders. It is publicity you can't buy, contributing to rebuild your client base.

It is good for everyone by any matrix, and not incompatible with profitability. If anything, it might propel your company to stand out from your competitors. I went forward and proposed a message to communicate: normally, we take care of your health starting with your teeth, but those are not normal times. While we cannot take care of your teeth, we thought of supporting initiatives that benefit our communities. We are XYZ industry leaders in our field and partners of the communities we do business in!

"Overcoming poverty is not an act of charity, it's an act of justice."
Nelson Mandela

Corporations are demanding justice from the government's measures. They are doing so for their survival, maintaining profits and jobs for their employees, their families and for the other companies who in turn sell products to them to ensure their own survival, as well as their employees and their families. It is all interconnected, and if we invest smartly in the weakest links, we will have a stronger community to come back to.

By tradition, it's been a common belief that profits, charity and ethics are sitting in opposite directions in the business world. Shareholders' first concern is profit maximization and at first glance, investing in the community seems to go against that objective.

The interest of the community and social values pose no threat to profit maximization of any healthy corporations. The examples are numerous. Providing services that are relevant to your industry will raise the awareness for your cause, your company and all the stakeholders.

From my conversations, I realized that my arguments came as a surprise and that it appeared conflictive with respect to what, in their minds, was an immediate need. But my track record had earned me their respect, and I was confident that it would stir things up. This is how we create good change.

In turn, they proposed ideas such as creating initiatives to offer free health care services to front line health care workers in need. This was a good first step because I got them to think differently. Now, I would need to ensure follow-up and maintain positive pressure to generate more ideas and come to generate results.

The following took place in my head and was not part of the conversation. My numbers speak for themselves, and I know I am an important client. While I had no formal decisional power with respect to their decision, corporate leaders would actually try to please me, or at least, not directly oppose me.

This was crucial. I felt I was a stakeholder who also was informally representing a larger base of stakeholders, and my opinion mattered to them. I have a profound respect for the challenges they were facing. However, I had to respect my values, as a stakeholder, and their decisions could motivate me to look for a better fit for me.

At the time of writing these lines, they haven't reached a decision yet. I believe more discussions are to follow. I believe in the critical importance of cohesion to promote a more sustainable way of doing business. There is no way they did not know this.

After all, it was not the first time that I solicited their participation in events that I organized, and they had participated before. I am simply true to my **WHY** even in challenging times.

This is **AFTERMATH - BUSINESS AFTER THE GREAT PAUSE.**

In time of crisis,
It is the perfect opportunity
To reinvent who we are.
Dr. BAK NGUYEN

CHAPTER 13
"THE LEVERAGE TO MATTER"
by Dr. BAK NGUYEN

We, business people, are people of leverage. Throughout our career, we master the work ethic to always go beyond what is expected of us and to never give up.

With time and experience, we found a niche where our talents are put to good use, very good use, and to serve our peers, the community and Society as a whole. This is how we've successfully built our organizations and became relevant. In other words, how we became rich.

Our power does not come from the money we yield, but the people we serve and the people looking up to us for guidance. Yes, we are officers of Society. Our role is to lead and keep the effort going. The more people we touch, the more important we are.

Those amongst us who are very successful are those who found a way to leverage their resources and themselves to do more and better with less until they have all the resources coming with success. This when they grow as an essential part of their Society, as a must in the lives of the target market.

So, in our line of logic, we matter every day, that why we are relevant and have the means to make the difference. In a global crisis like **THE VIRUS** where most people are put on the sidelines, what do we do?

Well, in the light of the past events, we saw companies like Tesla, Dyson, Nike and Apple find ways to serve the war effort against the virus, converting their factories to produce the much needed medical devices and furniture.

Even fashion industry leader Giorgio Armani is leading the way, offering his infrastructures and workforce to make medical overall. He did not wait for people or authorities to ask him for his contribution, he found his relevancy in the new fight.

Just like Bill Gates and Elon Musk, those are leaders because they took the challenge to reinvent themselves to where they were needed. Where Giorgio Armani converted his resources, Elon Musk gave his talent to drive change and put his teams and factories in contribution. The millions of Bill Gates took care of matters our government found too trivial to allocate the needed resources.

These great people are leaders and heroes reinventing themselves in times of needs. They may have reinvented themselves, but they did so being themselves and leveraging on what they know and understand better: driving change, identifying a need and to provide a solution. Doing what they do best is leveraging.

"Adapting their mastery to the present and immediate need is reinventing themselves."
Dr. Bak Nguyen

And why is it the best time to do so? Because there is no resistance! Most change are welcome with open arms. Well, this is the power each of us has, the mastery to do more with less and to reallocate resources. We do so with the will to make a difference and to matter, but we are also doing so, if we want to be successful, being true to our character and skillsets.

So how does it feel to be left on the sideline in the midst of this **VIRUS** crisis? How does it feel to be forced on pause? Please, don't take the question as an insult, but as an opener. We should contribute, we all do, not everywhere, but where we can matter the most, where we have leverage.

Well, we will win war, in time. The victory is mainly due because the war had unprecedented press, political and medical coverage, and monopolized all the attention of humankind. It monopolized all the attention, but not the resources, that while most of the people were left idle waiting on the sidelines.

Now, can you see what will happen without such coverage? We would be busy going back to our usual lives, and as the time we realized that the enemy is at our doors, it will be to capitulate.

Well, this is how we look at most of the issues our world and era face. Unfortunately or fortunately, all issues do not have as much political, press and media coverage. It does not mean that they aren't worth our attention or time. That surely doesn't mean that they do not matter or even exist! And who can make a difference about them?

It always started with a passionate victim or expert, exposing the vulnerability of our Society facing a void. Then, the media and politic class will decide if there is a scoop to be capitalized on and a campaign to be raised. If it does not comes with a viral effect, thin are the chances of global mobilization.

Is global warming less an issue of importance than THE VIRUS? Is the world hunger, the commerce of organs, the rights of women to abortion, the right to education, the research for cancer, the needs of the veterans, what is more important?

This is our cue, this is where philanthropy takes over. Before THE VIRUS, Bill Gates was a billionaire putting his fortune in the service of philanthropy. Well, today, he is leading the charge and the attention, in other words, influence.

Philanthropy is our call to power, to matter and to leverage our mastery, skillset and resources. Philanthropy is our chance to take a role of significance before the war reaches our shore. We act and contribute with the hope to never see that war coming.

Philanthropy is our chance to make a difference, to choose how we will matter and never to be left on the sideline again. Remember how it felt in the **GREAT PAUSE**? Never again.

"Philanthropy is not charity."
Dr. Bak Nguyen

Well, which is your cause? Will you act before the enemy reach our shore? Will you act before crying the blood and death of those close to you? Will you wait for the next political crisis, press coverage and humanitarian emergency? Better late than never, but we know better.

"The best leverages are the ones we put in place much before the facts, those we provoked and saw coming, not the one we have to react and improve on."

Dr. Bak Nguyen

So this is our chance to act before the crisis. The fact that there is no coverage is our chance to take a role of importance, not throwing ourself hoping for the best, but leveraging upon our mastery, skillsets and resources to coordinate a victory, not a war effort. This is philanthropy, our chance to matter.

If anything THE VIRUS has reminded us how fragile our Society and economy are. How quickly a life can fade away and how small is the world. But most importantly, how it felt to be left on the sideline. How costly and hard it was to improvise and react. Never again!

So where will you look at? Where will you aim your attention and make a stand, make a difference? You do not have to choose, you only have to open your heart and follow your instincts. With the blueprints from this book, you matter while keeping doing things the way you excel at. It is almost **to matter in auto-pilot**, once you have taken the time to implement a small change, a core change.

Philanthropy is your best deal, your leverage and your chance to be more than what you already are. Aren't we all not looking for our next challenges?

"Philanthropy is not a dare nor a challenge,
but leverage to matter."
Dr. Bak Nguyen

And please, do not simply throw yourself on the field looking for adventure and excitement. You are not a foot soldier. If you are reading this book, is because you are a general and an officer of Society with resources, organizations and a workforce at your command.

Leverage them, all of them, to lead change, leveraged and needed change.

"Success comes from the mastery of leveraging.
Philanthropy is our best leverage to matter."
Dr. Bak Nguyen

Never again. Never again will we wait and be left on the sidelines. Never again, we will wait for the enemy and the menace to reach our shore first. Never again will we allow ourselves to be surprised.

Choose your front and, in the name of Humankind, I thank you for your service and contribution to the evolution and prosperity of us all.

This is the information age, the rise of the millennials and the reign of social media.

This is **AFTERMATH - BUSINESS AFTER THE GREAT PAUSE.**

In time of crisis,
It is the perfect opportunity
To reinvent who we are.
Dr. BAK NGUYEN

CHAPTER 14

"FROM WITHIN"

by Dr. ERIC LACOSTE

"The grass isn't always greener on the other side;
the grass is greener where you water it."
Robert Fulghum

Since the beginning of this crisis, my clinic is on a standstill. As an individual, my body and my mind are resting well as much as this is possible! I have designed a least 10 different scenarios of the aftermath. What will I do and how will I do it? All of it while trying to stay true to my original purpose, to my **WHY**! At times, it is not easy, but I have no valid reasons to complain.

Before everything else, I define myself as a health care professional in a broader sense. What drives me is to take care of people in a larger sense as well. From a procedural standpoint, my profession is highly repetitive. I have placed more dental implants, done more soft tissue and bone grafts than I can count among other procedures.

What drives me to go back every day is the fact that I care for people. That's not repetitive at all because my patients are unique and present different challenges.

I built different levels of relationship and trust; managed different levels of anxiety etc.... The goal remains simple: to take care of others. This is how I keep my interest. I care about my staff, not only for who they are, but also because they bought into my mission.

I owe it to them to be the best possible leader. I continuously work to improve my leadership. I always believed that being a leader is a privilege that far exceeds the notion of being the majority owner of any company.

Most people I meet said that they could do what they wanted because it was their businesses! This kind of people are, with little to no exceptions, the worst kind of leaders. Real leaders serve others, they serve their employees, their patients and customers, they serve their team and investors alike.

> "I never lose. I either win or learn."
> Nelson Mandela

Collectively most will agree that we are facing an unprecedented threat, yet many historical events are there to inspire us.

Arguably, Nelson Mandela is one of the greatest leaders of all times. Never forgetting his **WHY** despite 27 years of imprisonment in difficult conditions. Compare to him, by no metrics, was I in real trouble!

In normal circumstances, my mission would propel me forward. Why should it be any different now? Regardless of the context, why should my mission be different? The plan cannot be fine tuned; there are still too many unknowns. Nevertheless, my entrepreneurial nature is pushing me to be ready.

My staffs don't need a boss, they need a leader: I must stand up.

In these times, I believe it is important to reach out to them, to make sure they are ok, answer any questions they might have, address their concerns, show my support and more importantly be accessible.

I believe that no matter how small or how large the organization, making everyone feels unique and that they each have a role to play is a crucial ingredient of success.

"Leaders eat last."
Simon Sinek

This has never been more true than today!! Without them, there is no business. It's easy to say, but when you actually show it, you have the power to impact your organizational dynamic in unsuspected ways!

After touching base individually with each of them, I realized that they had formed their own google meeting group and resolved many little issues on their own. I was actually behind or was I? Was this the result of our culture? I really hope so!

Nevertheless, at a time where many things could pull them away from the job and their co-workers, they spontaneously felt the need to regroup and to keep in touch. Their objective was not to discuss clinic's loss. It was to keep their sense of belonging and to stay connected to their why. This was a powerful message sent by a very small community.

Countless articles have been written about organizational culture! Yet a really good one remains a challenge for so many companies at all levels.

The few organizations that truly develop a culture have a better chance to dominate their industry and to develop a strong brand image. Studies show with little to no exception, that these companies have a clear understanding of their purpose.

Furthermore, they understand their costumers, they are selling much more than an image, and they are selfless with their products. Ideally, they partner up with their customers.

With this in mind, I told myself that there could be no better timing to discuss this with my team. Stuck in our daily activities, it had been a long time since we had done this. Way too long.

The discussion was held in an unfamiliar context. We don't usually do remote work. This was great because it removed many of the usual inhibitors that affect some. I was no longer a boss. I was the leader of a group, and I too, would have an opportunity to look at myself from the outside.

It is a humbling experience that led to great and genuine answers. I recommend this to all entrepreneurs, managers, CEO, and leaders. Everyone in your organization counts and many see things that you don't. It is a great opportunity to listen and to build better foundations.

"It's better to lead from behind and put others in front, when you celebrate victories and when nice things occur. You take the front line when there is danger. The people will appreciate your leadership. "
Nelson Mandela

My first meeting allowed me to see small things I didn't see anymore but were essential ingredients of my success. Never forget that success is also a trap and may blind you down the road. What you don't see or refuse to see, will be your downfall.

With this in hand, I was able to set up different scenarios to resume my professional activities, restructure some of our operations, plan for the staff return as well as define strategies to jump-start the process. More importantly, I was reminded all the little details of my differentiation of my competitive edge.

It is no big secret, One patient at a time, we team up to achieve the best treatment outcome possible. The same principles apply to my community: to find a way, one problem at a time. This is a mindset that should never be compromised.

On leadership, I believe it requires a clear purpose but also a good balance. I believe that the best employees don't miss their son's hockey game, school music recitals or doctor's appointments. I can count on one hand the number of events that I missed from my three sons combined. Most of those times were related to schedule conflict between them.

I like to give the same leeway to my staff members so that they do to miss events important to them and their loved ones. This, however, comes with great responsibility because we owe it to our patients to be meeting their needs.

As such, it is a transfer of leadership from me to them and from them to our patients. It is not perfect, and it requires some adjustments. We are making those adjustments so that we can convey the same message.

As a general rule, I believe that in the long run, the output of any team is directly impacted by the input of the leaders. In other words, the more you invest, the more you communicate effectively, the more the **WHY** of your organization will resonate at any level.

The **COVID** pause brings a beautiful opportunity to reflect on that for yourself and for your organization. It does not start with the outside. It starts from within.

This is **AFTERMATH - BUSINESS AFTER THE GREAT PAUSE.**

In time of crisis,
It is the perfect opportunity
To reinvent who we are.
Dr. BAK NGUYEN

CHAPTER 15

"BECAUSE WE CAN"

by Dr. BAK NGUYEN

This book has been written in the midst of **THE VIRUS** and from the cell of confinement. I never met in person my friend and co-author Eric Lacoste. But I can tell you that our friendship is genuine.

As soon as this war against the invisible enemy is won, we will share a glass and a great talk, face to face. If I've learned anything through this crisis and unique unreal world event, is that the world is such a small place, but our hearts don't have to be.

I opened up and reached out with the hope of saving all of us from a global economic recession. People responded, not all, but amongst those who did, we were amongst peers, thinkers, heroes.

Some had experience of crisis, some in politics, some in technology and some, like Eric, in philanthropy. I remembered how open and genuine he was, accepting my invitation for an interview on his perspective on this crisis.

Then, a few days later, I got an invite from him. He suggested another interview, one with the head of the philanthropic organization he was involved in. I remembered that I scratched my head, wandering if that can be included in my mission. I was out to save the economy and to save our industry. Philanthropy?!

A few days ago, I got feedback from a party that I was seeking help from for the salvation of my industry. I remembered his words and comments: "Who mandated you? Aren't you taking too much over your small shoulders?" Absolutely, small! The real word was even more condescending. And this is coming from a party usually seeking the business of my company. I remained polite, but the feeling stuck.

One impossible thing at a time! I was out already for two! Then again, should I take advices from smaller minds and smaller hearts? And what about him, Eric, Dr. Lacoste, when he accepted my invitation? I had to stay open and to listen.

So I went out of my way and schedule, by his request, an interview for him and the head of the philanthropy. We had a great recorded exchange in which they explained their vocation, who benefit from their actions, their challenges, even their failures.

"Being genuine and open have very strong side effects."
Dr. Bak Nguyen

I had no agenda, I was just open and followed the conversation. But being who I am, I targeted the issues I could see and lent them my head and imagination for a few minutes. Then I heard myself speaking on air about the promise that I was making to help leverage them.

I was the one saying those words, but I was as surprised and shocked by its content. This is how this book came along. I promised them a book, within 2 weeks so they can leverage themselves, even in the midst of the *WAR* and

GREAT PAUSE.

As soon as I finished the interview, I started regretting being so open. I told you that my training is on society and leverage. On the field, I could help, but with no leverage and maybe even handicaps. I needed a way to twist this into something my mind can process.

This is how I came back on the words I said in a previous communication where I laid down an initial salvation plan for the dental industry at the light of my first week of interviews, including the one with Dr. Lacoste. I said that if we, dentists, open our heart a little, we might have patients filling our schedule as this crisis unravel. Well, I did just that, opening my heart.

And then, it all came together. Instead of empowering Dr. Lacoste local initiative and lending him some exposure, what if I lend him my best platform, me? I wrapped my mind on the why and the how, not of helping one organization, but on fixing the need that these organizations have by not having the necessary means.

To be blunt, they don't know how to sell themselves. Selling is evil to them. On the other hand, I am so grateful to have kind-hearted people like them on the ground so I can keep doing what I do best! When I thanked them, it was from the bottom of my heart, just like when I mentioned my shame listening to them.

Can such differences be conciliated? Then, I remembered my friend and mentor, Dr. Jean De Serres, opening our book, **THE RISE OF THE UNICORN**, saying that our friendship was built on difference, the respect of that difference and how we are building from that difference.

So that's what I did. To build using my difference. Different points of view, different tools, different leverage and especially, a different public, you! Most authors before me will pledge for the nobility, the need and the magnitude of helping the world and those in need.

Well, as good as it may sound, if you are still reading this book by now, it meant that the message faded sooner than the needs. I have zero tolerance for those talking and telling people what to do! I can stand those people thinking that they know better. I trust people who do, them I follow. I connect, become friends and help when they ask. Well, they did.

"Philanthropy is not charity."
Dr. Bak Nguyen

So I have 2 weeks to find and execute a leverage in philanthropy, a world new to me, while still surfing the panic and fear, trying to save the economy and my industry with my stripes as a dentist. Are my shoulders that small? I used that reminder to fuel my passion!

Philanthropy is not charity, what if it can be a leverage? The only way I know how to succeed is to bet it all. So I did, I put this promise at the heart of my attention, using the time and resources I had to find a way to save my own company out of this critical pause... my company is in great shape, I was in expansion mode when we got hit by **THE VIRUS**.

Expansion also means exposure, great exposure! I could have close down on my misery and beg for help. Instead, I chose to open up and to help my team and peers instead. Doing so, I was still in trouble, but at least, I was doing what I do best, to leverage and to find constructive solutions.

"Great ideas are built from great differences."
Dr. Jean De Serres

And I started working. More than encouraging and helping Dr. Lacoste to start his own writing career, I used this book as a prelude to how I would rewrite my business proposal. I am risking an all in! And for what?

"Standing at the edge, I didn't ask myself what I had to lose, but how long I had to score another win…"
Dr. Bak Nguyen

I am writing the last and final chapter of this book. I can also tell you that I have the best, most eloquent, comprehensive and articulate business proposal I had ever produced.

Rewriting the philosophy of my own industry to address its voids and blind angles, leveraging on the needs that this crisis has amplified in all of our societies and proposing a quick but lasting fix from a unique point of service.

I multiplied my ask for the initial round of financing by an X factor that would shock most of you. I borrowed the eloquence from philanthropy, this added to my leadership taking care of my own (peers and industry) added up to my strategies and tactics to make it one of the most profitable endeavor ever proposed in my field.

I even borrowed from philanthropy and society its means. Talking to people, I had to make interviews and videos. Write books and speeches, and then, reading them in audiobooks or podcasts.

Well, I borrowed from that glam to leverage my our endeavor: my business plan was supposed to be a one-pager, instead, I had 30 minutes of speech recorded into videos and edited Hollywood style, Dr. Bak's style.

Then, we put them into a web one-pager, the text presenting the fact and numbers, the videos, giving the context and spirit. I will still produce that one-pager, but it will serve more as a teaser to lead to this interactive presentation of the future instead of leading to a spreadsheet, expensive and generic, made by people thinking that my shoulders were small...

I am still fighting for the future of my vision and company. I still have to convince my board and the board directors of all the banks and investment firms, but never before I felt more ready, eloquent and right on point. I will get everyone richer and happier, even those I don't know the names and who have no idea of my existence yet.

This is what I meant with: **BECAUSE I CAN**. Even this book can have a great future. What started as a promise in the heat of generosity became a new angle of leveraging, both economic and social. I am looking for the attention of the UN General Secretary Africa to have her views on the content of this book and how it could help the **United Nations** to further the expansion of the **UN GLOBAL COMPACT** for a better world.

"I listened with my heart, built with my GREED and executed leveraging from the differences."
Dr. Bak Nguyen

If you never heard of me again, that would be because I died fighting at the front. But I highly doubt that. I was exposed and vulnerable as I started this endeavor and my confinement. I am now stronger than ever because I built from the differences.

I will say it again, philanthropy is not charity. Try it, you might even find bigger leverages than I had!

I woke up this morning reading comments made about M. Benzos, the richest man alive giving 100M to help relieve hunger in this unique time of crisis. People were saying that it was a small price to pay for his public image and persona. Although I understood what they meant, it also reminded me words of Robert Kiyosaki about how poor people say that rich people are greedy.

If everyone had a PR image to fix as M. Bezos, we would have no more world hunger to worry about! So who cares what they think! I salute M. Bezos for his actions, no matter his motivation. He did it because he could! So can we all!

I am more than hopeful. I now stand strong and flexible, insightful and influential because I built from the differences. I chose to open my heart, and my head expanded. And so followed my reach and power.

How far will you expand yours? If people were fighting at the glass ceiling, I found a way to use it as my floor and foundation. I started before with the affirmation: **CHANGING THE WORLD FROM A DENTAL CHAIR**, then, I had to prove my word to the world.

That's how I gained the favor of the financial world.

Can you imagine what would come next? My closing on the new Mdex & Co's financial proposal is now **BECAUSE WE ARE THE FOUNDATION OF THE INDUSTRY.**

I could never say such words if I did not open up and built from the difference; if I did not put my leveraging skill at the service of philanthropy and society. I am still a bold leader and a visionary walking his words. I now have more words to ride on. What are yours?

You are rich, because you did.
You make a difference, because you care.
You make it last, because this is who you are,
Builders of the world.

We do all of that because we can!
And we have fun doing so.
Scoring over the glass ceiling!

This is the information age, the rise of the millennials and the reign of social media.

This is **AFTERMATH - BUSINESS AFTER THE GREAT PAUSE.**

P.S.: And my business proposal and the foundation of the industry? Watch me!

In time of crisis,
It is the perfect opportunity
To reinvent who we are.
Dr. BAK NGUYEN

CHAPTER 16
"DIFFERENCE MAKER"
by Dr. ERIC LACOSTE

Many times in my life I have been consumed by doubts. Doubts create a feeling of uncertainty that lead you to act with a lack of conviction or worst, that places you in a state of completely inertia.

Profound doubt is the first feeling that came to me when Dr. Bak first proposed the idea to co-write this book. I had never envisioned myself writing a book. That said, if there is one thing I have learned about doubt: if you let it consume you for too long, it will stall everything. The more time passes by, the heavier your feet become. It's the nature of things.

"Some people want it to happen, some wish it would happen, others make it happen."
Michael Jordan

When meeting with a challenge, a smart one, I usually find the willpower and energy within to respond in kind. Writing a book would bring me out of my comfort zone. I had no doubt that I was carrying an important message that deserves, no, that needs, to be heard.

At times, I wished I could have someone famous to deliver the message, but fate brought it to my feet. It was my walk to take, my talk to embrace. It was my own responsibility to find a way to leave no doubt as to its relevance and importance.

"Where we are met with cynicism and doubts and those who tell us that we can't, we will respond with that timeless creed that sums up the spirit of a people: Yes, we can."
Barack Obama

When I think of it, writing this book is an exercise about taking ownership of my purpose, of my **WHY**. It's a commitment. It's written and published for anyone to read. It's about being true to my principles:

1. To conduct business ethically, responsibly and sustainably
2. To be aligned with the best practices in business

3. To promote positive leadership
4. Strive to offer the best possible patient cares
5. To work positively with all stakeholders
6. To be actively involved in my community and work for its benefits
7. To promote dental and systemic health
8. To promote education and physical activity
9. To fight poverty and promote a better social justice
10. To always keep improving

As I am writing these final words, some parts of the world is getting ready to face the eye of the storm while other parts are preparing to move towards the post **COVID** era. No one can really say how this crisis will change the course of the future. Nevertheless, it precipitated discussions, raised questions and hopefully will create sustainable changes.

THE VIRUS aligned everyone's interests across industries and irrespectively of social status. Health became a universal concern. People wishing others to stay healthy on a routine basis as if it was New Year's every day.

The enemy is a virus, not another political party, neither a religious or economic ideology. There is something beautiful in this. Earth is our only home and, the last I checked, the International Space Station has only room for 6 people. If that is not enough for us to collectively start thinking differently? I don't know what is.

My message is one of unity; it is a call to action for corporate members, entrepreneurs and professionals across the board. Together, let's generate more wealth but let us build sustainably all while working towards better social justice. By taking care of the most vulnerable of our communities, we will secure a better tomorrow for younger generations, for our future.

Personally, I will contribute my best and my all, working with Dr. Bak and others to help shape the future of my industry. I will do so cautiously and always with respect to my values aligned with sustainable development. I will also continue to multiply my initiatives to help my community grow stronger.

I also want to reach out to anyone who wishes to do more. It may simply be exchanging idea, providing advices, speaking at a conference or building a project together. Please feel welcome to contact me. By joining forces maybe we can become the difference-makers and bring the attribute to a whole new level.

As I remain grateful for what I have and how it allows me to contribute the way I had, I will continue to seek new opportunities, to build more, to learn more and to keep improving.

The journey is far from over.Very humbly, I wish to inspire people and hope that someone will look at me and say: Because of you I contributed to make my community better.

"Your voice can change the world."
Eric Lacoste

This is **AFTERMATH - BUSINESS AFTER THE GREAT PAUSE.**

CONCLUSION
"MY PLEA"
by Dr. BAK NGUYEN

This has been a crazy ride, one I did not see coming. I started this endeavor out of politeness, life on-air as with we were on an interview. That was less than two weeks ago. 34K words later, opening the door to a newfound friend and helping him to write his first book, here we are, at the conclusion.

What started as a promise that I could have regretted, took at life on its own and disproportional weight in my mind and my conscience. Writing, I said everything I had in mind right in the first chapter. Then, I knew that I could keep going, but by the fourth chapter, I will run out of ideas and words. That's not what happened.

I wrote and got much pleasure to see Eric keeping up with my pace. That's the how, but in essence, the text drafted itself, provoking events and changes in my own life. All I had to do was to report them. This is how I understood the importance of this issue: to leverage the crisis to rebuild, better and with sustainability.

Somewhere, the values were laying dormant in me. All it took was a chance to reflect and to express these values. I am a builder of my society and a good doctor. I genuinely care for people and for society, but have I done enough? This book and its consequences over my own life proved to me how shy I was on my initiative.

I mixed ambitions and greed with nobility and vision and this is what came out. Not only a book, not just a friendship but the best business plan I've never written, one that, if accepted, will put me years ahead of my precedent version. And you know what? The odds of being accepted are much, much more in my favor now that I gave it a true meaning of **SOCIETY**.

I may be a visionary and a dreamer, but I learned, a long time ago, that nothing can be done being naive. I believe in my ideas and my words, but I also know that to achieve concrete results, lasting results, I must appeal to what's important to any of us.

So I embraced my ambition and built. I leveraged my greed and my position to build bigger, broader, better. This is who I am, a builder. So are each of you, builders of society. We have our goals and priorities, we know have to adapt to surf the storm.

This is not a storm, it is the **GREAT PAUSE**, but it is not the end. If anything, it is our chance to find solid footing to jump once more and to flirt with the possibilities, the forgotten, of what can be both our legacy and destiny.

"On the tracks, we are efficient. At the GREAT PAUSE, we can now be unstoppable, even out of the tracks."
Dr. Bak Nguyen

Even if this book has been written with the intention of making the world a better place, of promoting a better social justice, of writing the wrongs, if there is one thing that I hate is someone telling me what to do, and even worst, how to do it. So I won't be that person!

What I did in here was nothing more than to share with you another episode of my evolution, of how I opened my heart and find a cause to help, and from that cause, by my actions, I found the ultimate leverage for my own ambition and business.

Say that I did it for me, say that I am selfish, say what you must! If all of us fixed their image problem as Jeff Bezos did, there will be no more world hunger! I salute his generosity and thank him for leading the way. If anything, he showed us all that one can do much without having to sacrifice too much!

"God made us all unique and different.
We each have a different key to ignite.
Ours is Greed, in a better word, ambition."
Dr. Bak Nguyen

I am many things, but a hypocrite isn't one of them. I succeeded the day I accepted and embraced who I am and leveraged that ever since. You have my steps, my motives and, hopefully, will read about its consequences in the near future. But now that I wrote them down, I will either succeed or die trying, that you already know.

I will get a copy of this book to the United Nations, to the people I know. I am proposing the amendments to my business proposal to my board and investors as we speak. I am unveiling my plans to my team and to the rest of the world, only, you had a first peak.

It is not my final results that should intrigue you, but my thought process and my leveraging mechanisms. If you are still reading these lines, it means that you are feeling the rise coming, your rise, a new angle to sprint on as soon as the pause is waved. That's your ability to leverage.

Not doing it will leave so much potential going to waste. This is what I answered to Eric as he was surprised by my degree of commitment to redraft my own business plan. I could lose it all if the board and the investors think that I am nuts and that the confinement had the best of me. I can also rise very fast and go very far, outside of the tracks! It is a well-calculated risk.

Isn't that exciting? Isn't that what we thrive for, all of our lives? To do the impossible and to *find a way* where no one expected? This is our chance. Our chance to reinvent ourselves, our chance to rise higher, bigger, bolder with less resistance, our chance to nobility and to a greater destiny.

All of that while increasing our chance of success and reducing the risk. What kind of odds were you facing before? Don't tell me that those aren't worth your time!

"Yes we can, we can have it all."
Dr. Bak Nguyen

And once we understood that everything is within reach, it suddenly becomes simpler, easier. This is abundance, the state of abundance. **ABUNDANCE** is not given to anyone looking at himself since he will miss the horizon looking down at his bellybutton.

Abundance is accessible when one looks up and see beyond the horizon. This is where justice, peace and prosperity lay.

We are masters in the art of leveraging. Just like we knew that money as no odor, our motives aren't what will weight in the balance, but our results and its consequences will. I love that word: consequences. Neither positive nor negative, but it has weight. And what is a consequence but the result of our choices and actions?

We are drivers and doers, not talkers. In this **GREAT PAUSE**, we had the chance to be thinkers for a short while. Now it's the time to resume, to put back our suits and to jump in our racing cars to drive the world to a better future. This is who we are, we are winners, champions and makers of the worlds. We are difference-makers.

Where will you lead us? What do you reserve for all of us? I can't wait to see how better the world will be now that all of our interests are aligned, now that we had the chance to retune our leverage and minds toward the future, one where no one is left behind. Let's cut the anchors and rise, all together.

"I didn't need wings to fly,
just cutting my anchors."
Dr. Bak Nguyen

And those anchors are what we chose to forget, what we chose to ignore, what is still weighting our minds and heads before we go to sleep. If after 40 years there were still laying around, it must be a good reason. No more will they slow me down. Those dead weights are now the new cornerstones of my creation and the new fuel in my combustion chamber.

And once again, this is the essence of leveraging, to find a way where there was none.

"Find leverage out of each of your
liability to move forward."
Dr. Bak Nguyen

After 63 books, this quote still come up as the wisdom of the day! What started as a hesitant book, one that will stall after the 4 chapters, now refuses to lay down and let go. If I was committed to 8 chapters to respect the **NUMBER OF THE DRAGON**, one that will ensure the infinite success to this endeavor, your endeavor. Now, I have a hard time to let go.

Yup, I really have my both my feet and my head in abundance. And the feeling is a unique one. One where power and freedom is one. Where feeling tall and humble is the same, one where light and darkness come together.

The time for fighting is over. Now is a new age, one of abundance. Lead the way, you know how, you have the map and with leverage, show me the cheats!

Do good, do much, do what you are born to do and rise!

This is **AFTERMATH - BUSINESS AFTER THE GREAT PAUSE.**

In time of crisis,
It is the perfect opportunity
To reinvent who we are.
Dr. BAK NGUYEN

UAX

ULTIMATE AUDIO EXPERIENCE

A new way to learn and enjoy Audiobooks. Made to be entertaining while keeping the self-educational value of a book, UAX will appeal to both auditive and visual people. UAX is the blockbuster of the Audiobooks.

UAX will cover most of Dr. Bak's books, and is now negotiating to bring more authors and more titles to the UAX concept.

Now streaming on Spotify, Apple Music and available for download on all major music platforms. Give it a try today!

FROM THE SAME AUTHOR
Dr. Bak Nguyen

TITLES AVAILABLE AT
www.DrBakNguyen.com

MAJOR LEAGUES' ACCESS

FACTEUR HUMAIN
LE LEADERSHIP DU SUCCÈS
par DR BAK NGUYEN & CHRISTIAN TRUDEAU

ehappyPedia
THE RISE OF THE UNICORN
BY DR. BAK NGUYEN & DR. JEAN DE SERRES

CHAMPION MINDSET
LEARNING TO WIN
BY DR. BAK NGUYEN & CHRISTOPHE MULUMBA

BRANDING DR.BAK
BALANCING STRATEGY AND EMOTIONS
BY DR. BAK NGUYEN, BRENDA GARCIA & SANTIAGO CHICA

BUSINESS

La Symphonie des Sens
ENTREPREUNARIAT
par DR BAK NGUYEN

Industries Disruptors
BY DR. BAK NGUYEN, ROUBA SAKR AND COLLABORATORS

Changing the World from a dental chair
BY DR. BAK NGUYEN

The Power Behind the Alpha
BY TRANIE VO & DR. BAK NGUYEN

SELFMADE
GRATITUDE AND HUMILITY
BY DR. BAK NGUYEN

CHILDREN'S BOOK
with William Bak

The Trilogy of Legends

THE LEGEND OF THE CHICKEN HEART
BY DR. BAK NGUYEN & WILLIAM BAK

THE LEGEND OF THE LION HEART
BY DR. BAK NGUYEN & WILLIAM BAK

THE LEGEND OF THE DRAGON HEART
BY DR. BAK NGUYEN & WILLIAM BAK

WE ARE ALL DRAGONS
BY DR. BAK NGUYEN & WILLIAM BAK

The Collection of the Chicken

THE 9 SECRETS OF THE SMART CHICKEN
BY DR. BAK NGUYEN & WILLIAM BAK

THE SECRET OF THE FAST CHICKEN
BY DR. BAK NGUYEN & WILLIAM BAK

THE LEGEND OF THE SUPER CHICKEN
BY DR. BAK NGUYEN & WILLIAM BAK

THE STORY OF THE CHICKEN SHIT
BY DR. BAK NGUYEN & WILLIAM BAK

WHY CHICKEN CAN'T DREAM?
BY DR. BAK NGUYEN & WILLIAM BAK

THE STORY OF THE CHICKEN NUGGET
BY DR. BAK NGUYEN & WILLIAM BAK

IDENTITY
THE ANTHOLOGY OF QUESTS
BY DR. BAK NGUYEN

HYBRID
THE MODERN QUEST OF IDENTITY
BY DR. BAK NGUYEN

FORCES OF NATURE
FORGING THE CHARACTER OF WINNERS
BY DR. BAK NGUYEN

HORIZON, BUILDING UP THE VISION
VOLUME ONE
BY DR. BAK NGUYEN

HORIZON, ON THE FOOTSTEP OF TITANS
VOLUME TWO
BY DR. BAK NGUYEN

MOMENTUM TRANSFER
BY DR. BAK NGUYEN & Coach DINO MASSON

LEVERAGE
COMMUNICATION INTO SUCCESS
BY DR. BAK NGUYEN AND COLLABORATORS

THE POWER OF YES
MY 18 MONTHS JOURNEY
BY DR. BAK NGUYEN

HOW TO WRITE A BOOK IN 30 DAYS
BY DR. BAK NGUYEN

POWER
EMOTIONAL INTELLIGENCE
BY DR. BAK NGUYEN

MENTORS
BY DR. BAK NGUYEN

HOW TO NOT FAIL AS A DENTIST
BY DR. BAK NGUYEN

HOW TO WRITE A SUCCESSFUL BUSINESS PLAN
BY DR. BAK NGUYEN & ROUBA SAKR

MASTERMIND, 7 WAYS INTO THE BIG LEAGUE
BY DR. BAK NGUYEN & JONAS DIOP

PLAYBOOK INTRODUCTION
BY DR. BAK NGUYEN

PLAYBOOK INTRODUCTION 2
BY DR. BAK NGUYEN

SUCCESS IS A CHOICE
BLUEPRINTS FOR HEALTH PROFESSIONALS
BY DR. BAK NGUYEN

RISING
TO WIN MORE THAN YOU ARE AFRAID TO LOSE
BY DR. BAK NGUYEN

PARENTING

THE BOOK OF LEGENDS
BY DR. BAK NGUYEN & WILLIAM BAK

THE BOOK OF LEGENDS 2
BY DR. BAK NGUYEN & WILLIAM BAK

THE BOOK OF LEGENDS 3
THE END OF THE INNOCENCE AGE
BY DR. BAK NGUYEN & WILLIAM BAK

PERSONAL GROWTH

REBOOT
MIDLIFE CRISIS
BY DR. BAK NGUYEN

THE ENERGY FORMULA
BY DR. BAK NGUYEN

AMONGST THE ALPHA
BY DR. BAK NGUYEN & COACH JONAS DIOP

AMONGST THE ALPHA vol.2
ON THE OTHER SIDE
BY DR. BAK NGUYEN & COACH JONAS DIOP

THE 90 DAYS CHALLENGE
BY DR. BAK NGUYEN

PHILOSOPHY

LEADERSHIP
PANDORA'S BOX
BY DR. BAK NGUYEN

KRYPTO
TO SAVE THE WORLD
BY DR. BAK NGUYEN & ILYAS BAKOUCH

SOCIETY

PROFESSION HEALTH
THE UNCONVENTIONAL QUEST OF HAPPINESS
BY DR. BAK NGUYEN, DR. MIRJANA SINDOLIC,
DR. ROBERT DURAND AND COLLABORATORS

WHITE COATS
THE UNCONVENTIONAL QUEST OF HAPPINESS

DR.

Bob Nguyen

www.ingramcontent.com/pod-product-compliance
Lightning Source LLC
Chambersburg PA
CBHW070309200326
41518CB00010B/1940